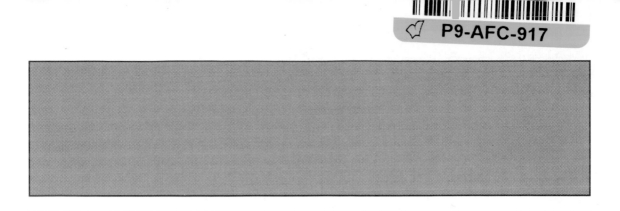

One Square Mile on the Atlantic Coast

Wall Township

South Arm

Musquash Cove

Northeast Arm

Memorial Park

Neptune City

Belmar

Shark River, New Jersey

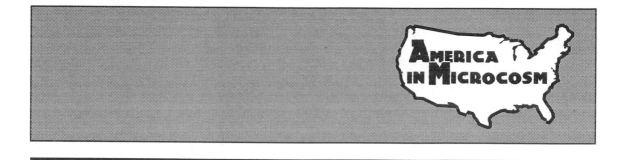

AMERICA IN MICROCOSM

One Square Mile on the Atlantic Coast

An Artist's Journal of the New Jersey Shore

JOHN R. QUINN

Walker and Company   New York

For Luci
"Her ways are pleasant ways, and all her paths are peace."
—Proverbs 3:17

First published in the United States of America in 1993 by Walker Publishing Company, Inc.

Published simultaneously in Canada by Thomas Allen & Son
Canada, Limited, Markham, Ontario

Library of Congress Cataloging-in-Publication Data
Quinn, John R.
One square mile on the Atlantic coast: an artist's journal of the
New Jersey shore / John R. Quinn
p.   cm.—(America in microcosm series)
Includes bibiographical references and index.
ISBN 0-8207-7395-8
1. Estuarine ecology—New Jersey—Shark River Estuary.   2. Coastal
ecology—New Jersey—Shark River Estuary.   3. Natural history—New
Jersey.   I. Title.   II. Series: America in microcosm.
QH105.N5Q56   1993
508.749'09146—dc20   92-36518
                                                          CIP

Book Design by Georg Brewer
Printed in the United States of America

2   4   6   8   10   9   7   5   3   1

The quotation from the writings of Elizabeth Coatsworth that appears on page v is from her book *Maine Memories* published by The Countryman Press, Woodstock, Vermont. It is included here courtesy of The Countryman Press.

And if Americans are to become really at home in America it must be through the devotion of many people to many small, deeply loved places. The field by the sea, the single mountain peak seen from a man's door, the island of trees and farm buildings in the western wheat, must be sung and painted and praised until each takes on the gentleness of the thing long loved, and becomes an unconscious part of us and we of it.

—Elizabeth Coatsworth

Contents

Acknowledgments

A book, like a habitat, is a multifaceted collection of impressions and individuals doing their special things, the sum of it all wrapped within a cover that presents itself to the observer in a pleasing and rewarding way. I cannot, of course, adequately communicate my gratitude to those numberless members of the natural world that comprise the warp and weave of my New Jersey square mile. But I can indeed make use of the language to offer special thanks and expressions of grateful appreciation to: my editor, Mary Kennan Herbert, who invited me to share my special part of New Jersey's fabled shore with others, something I'd long wanted to do, and then patiently and unerringly piloted me past the shoals and sandbars and finally through the channels of its safe passage into a finished journal. And to Jim Johnson and Matthew Rusher, Neptune City boys both, who grew up by the riverside and remember it well, for shared reminiscences and contributed materials. And friend and colleague Jerry G. Walls, for giving the Appendix the scientific twice-over with his matchless editorial eye. And finally, to all the boat skippers and bait dealers and diggers, the anglers and game wardens, the bird watchers and fish watchers, the marina owners and bridge tenders, the local folk and the summertime "bennies"; in short, all the many and varied people who in their comings and goings make the Shark River estuary the intriguingly bittersweet little piece of nature it most assuredly is.

Foreword

The New Jersey shore is a genuine natural wonder. It is a source of pride and inspiration that delights us and renews our spirit. It is a place that we in New Jersey eagerly show off to visitors from around the country and abroad. Everyone, from young children coming to the shore for the first time to senior citizens who have lived their entire lives within earshot of the surf, can draw inspiration from the majestic scenery and plentiful wildlife. In recent years, the people of New Jersey have come together in realizing that the shore is also something to preserve and protect for those who come after us.

The future of the coastline is largely controlled by the way we set our priorities. Increasingly, we are learning to respect all aspects of our natural environment and to coexist with it. We are very proud that New Jersey is a national leader in recycling and that we've put an end to the ocean dumping of waste off the Jersey coast.

There will be many challenges ahead. Technology will help us, but technology alone won't be enough. We'll have to do a lot of planning and a lot of conservation. As I look to the future, I am confident. New Jerseyans are resourceful, creative, hardworking people, and there is nothing we can't do when we set our minds to it.

John R. Quinn has chosen a very special square mile of New Jersey as his subject, but this is not the only square mile that would have made a good choice. As governor, I feel very privileged to have the opportunity to travel across this great state and get to know many square miles of New Jersey. Among them there are countless that would reward the kind of thoughtful study that Mr. Quinn provides for the Shark River estuary in the pages of this book.

—Jim Florio, governor of New Jersey

Introduction

If there is one thing that can be said with any degree of certainty about the great state of New Jersey, it is that the roughly hourglass-shaped parcel of territory that lies between the broad Atlantic and the mighty Delaware River has proven to be highly popular with humankind. That this is a truism can be found in the fact that there are today more individuals of the genus *Homo*, species *sapiens*, to be found scattered throughout its 8,224.24 square miles—or 4,813,000 acres—than in any other place on the North American continent. The continental United States contains 3.539 million square miles of land surface area, or about 6 percent of the earth's total, and New Jersey has about 0.20 percent of that. But though it may be lilliputian, New Jersey, for better or for worse, is the most densely populated state in the Union.

Regardless of the state's aesthetic drawbacks, the "Jersey jokes," the aromatic oil refineries, and the organized chaos of the New Jersey Turnpike, the now euphemistically named "Garden State" has more people—close to eight million at last

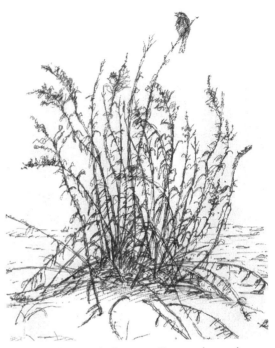

The subtle arrival of spring. *I sat in the sand on the ocean beach, roughing in the spare lines of a wind-dried clump of last year's seaside goldenrod, when a tiny fleck of animate life, a song sparrow, flitted in from the nearby dunes and alighted on the tallest sprig of the defunct plant. At once, it threw back its head and announced its presence to the world at large, its melodious and familiar refrain picked up by the sea wind and delivered up and down the beach, plainly heard above the roar and swash of the powerful surf.*

count—living within its borders than any other state or province except California, the once aptly named

A spindly, wind-dried staghorn sumac, perched on an isolated dune surrounded by beach grass. *This plant's tenuous anchorage had been cut off from the nearby upland by the high tides and surf of a fall storm, but its root system holds the shape of the dune; if the weather remains settled for the season, organic debris will settle in the depression behind the dune and terrestrial plants will soon recolonize the area. Another severe storm will, of course, further erode the dune and reclaim the spot as sloping, sandy, windblown beach.*

Golden State. Many of these residents are transients with no particular plans to end their days in Lords Carteret and Berkeley's former domain, but most are in fact here by choice. To them, New Jersey is home, and they accept that fact, along with the state's unfairly high standing on the regional jokes roster, with the candor, humor, resignation, and pride that is perhaps characteristic of, and unique to, the urbanized Northeast—where, after all, all those Brooklyn jokes had their genesis.

Authors Angus Gillespie and Michael Rockland expressed it well when they noted in their book *Looking for America on the New Jersey Turnpike* that New Jersey "is the ultimate suburban state—the place where the struggle between the machine and the garden has been joined and where a compromise of sorts has been struck between competing visions of America."

New Jersey is all too often held up as an example of the absolute worst in environmental calamity, a geographical monument to lack of forethought and planning. But the state was recently ranked fourteenth among the fifty for its determination to correct the ecological wrongs its inhabitants have wrought upon it over the decades. New Jersey's famous beaches, littered by trash, have made international headlines in recent years, but a massive and ultimately successful cleanup campaign was launched in 1989 and today the 127-mile-long "Jersey shore" once again emanates the almost mystical appeal that annually lures millions of visitors to that narrow sandy strand by the Atlantic.

Taken as a whole, the image of New Jersey as a place to experience nature in an untrammeled condition becomes increasingly difficult to justify. The state is simply too convenient to two great population centers—Philadelphia and New York City, both in other states—to escape the sprawling development and proliferating urban infrastructure required to accommodate this growing human throng. Throughout the booming 1980s, New Jersey lost an astounding 180,000 acres of natural habitat and farmland to urban and residential development. Wetland losses in the same period are estimated at about 22 percent of the 1985 figure of 900,000 acres. Unless there are radical changes in demographics and population growth, not to mention

environmental priorities among the populace at large, there is little likelihood that New Jersey will escape the fate that awaits most northeastern coastal states in the next century: that of a completely urbanized geographical and political entity with fragmented enclaves of intensively managed and heavily utilized natural areas.

In view of the state's less than rosy environmental outlook and generally negative public image, why, then, bother to chronicle its land and wildlife in drawings, paintings, or in any of the other arts? What of environmental, biological, artistic, or aesthetic merit and appeal can possibly be found in the world's largest suburb? The backwoods

A powerful storm surf assaulting the ocean beach near the mouth of the inlet. *The scene was one of wild confusion: the mountainous rollers crashing in upon the beach, the exuberance of the gulls as they jockeyed and swirled about in the near gale-force, southeast wind. I found myself hampered in my drawing efforts by the strong wind and its cargo of light rain/mist and so roughed in the lines of the incoming seas and the action of the birds with a few choice lines and then finished the drawing later.*

Entropy. *This scene, captured quickly in both the broad strokes of a permanent marker and the fine lines of a roller-point pen, acquired a somewhat ominous quality by the "Stonehengelike" wreckage of an old pier slowly collapsing into the sea.*

trailways and wilderness vistas of Alaska, Montana, or Saskatchewan would appear to provide infinitely more grist for the artist's brush or the writer's pen. But New Jersey?

As they say in Hoboken, "Fuhgedaboudit!"

But New Jersey, almost in spite of itself, does indeed have much to offer the aesthetic eye. The answer lies far from the hallowed chambers of commerce and won't be found within the artificial lines drawn on road maps or surveyors' blueprints. It has little or

nothing to do with New Jersey's popular image or with its undeserved write-off as the New York–Philadelphia "corridor state." Rather, it has much more to do with all those square miles—part of the very title of this book. Although roughly 46 percent of New Jersey's terrain has been converted or altered to some degree to suit the needs and requirements of its human inhabitants, roughly 80 percent of the population lives on a little more than 15 percent of the land area, and this mostly in the state's northeastern sector. Most of the remainder, though intensively agricultural or third- and fourth-growth forest, retains what could be called a "natural," or at least "rural," character. Sections of the famous Pine Barrens or of the more mountainous northwestern portion of the state are distant enough from the accoutrements of civilization to get lost in, though one is never more than five miles from a road anywhere in New Jersey. A random square mile in the Pines or in the Kitatinnies, taken as a whole unto itself, would present the interested investigator with a visual experience akin to that attained in much more sparsely peopled places.

But like it or not, New Jersey is at the center of the historic and fabled gateway to North America, and as such, it has been host to nonnative immigrants for more than three

First light at the edge of the sea. *Perhaps because the field of view is so much greater than in other habitats, and because the eastern horizon lends a stark, linear dimension to the rim of the world itself, dawn arrives here long before the sun actually makes its appearance.*

Unless one stands in the surf wash on the beach, the dawn watcher's view of the new day along much of the New Jersey coast is very likely to include manmade structures of one kind or another. Piers, jetties, and anchored boats are all a part of the modern shore scene, as are bridges, like this one. I sketched this "dawn's early light" view of the Ocean Avenue bridge from a bulkhead just up-channel. I used two pens: a "Sharpie" permanent marker, with broad, heavy strokes for rendering the deep shadows of the upper sky and the water in the foreground; and a Permaroller fine-line pen, for building up the values in the background and for drawing the structure itself.

hundred years. It also boasts a physical environment so rich and varied that, in spite of the way things ecological have turned out here, the region still offers a veritable galaxy of unique habitats as well as the organisms that call them home. The state boasts more than eight hundred lakes and ponds and about three hundred creeks and rivers, including roughly fourteen hundred miles of trout streams. Most of these waters are in at least fairly good shape, given the population density and

degree of development here. And polls indicate that the majority of the eight million residents of the state are intensely interested in what natural treasures the place still possesses in the 1990s and have a commendable desire to preserve what's left.

So the question asked must be: which of the eight thousand-plus square miles that comprise the state might prove most characteristic of the "natural" New Jersey, yet provide the reader with a glimpse of nature's riches

Dawn at the Ocean Avenue Bridge. *A little crowd of red-breasted mergansers heads seaward against an incoming tide. In the distance is the Avon boardwalk, jammed with strollers in summer but empty in February save for a few hardy joggers.*

to be found in a 5,280 square-foot section of a heavily populated region? One in which an estimated twelve hundred people live on an average square mile of land area?

A square mile of undisturbed Pinelands presents a picturesque sight, to be sure, but the habitat is not especially rich in biological diversity and is essentially duplicated in many places south along the Atlantic Coastal Plain. A close look at a parcel of mountainous terrain in Warren or Sussex counties would be both varied and interesting, but the scene would be virtually interchangeable with one in

nearby Bucks County, Pennsylvania, or Orange County in upstate New York. The broad Hackensack River meadowlands in northern New Jersey have been chronicled as both an environmental disaster and a model of ecosystem recovery after the fact. But this beleaguered habitat, home of the sprawling Meadowlands Sports Complex, numberless industrial plants, and several major traffic arteries including the famous New Jersey Turnpike, is essentially a disturbed environment dominated by the

The roost. *As the sun rose well above the sea and the full light of day arrived at the inlet, I moved to the south end of the bridge and stood in the middle of its northbound lane to capture a quick sketch of the still relatively carless roadway with the ocean to the right. After I had roughed in the drawing, I noticed that the resident street pigeons were exuberantly departing their nocturnal roosts beneath the structure and trading back and forth in the swift, direct flight characteristic of all pigeons and doves. There were a great many of them and their fleet forms were always in view, so I was able to simply study the flights for a time and then add a rough sketch of the birds to the drawing almost from memory.*

SHARK River Hills Marina

The north cove of the estuary. *Fed by a rather feeble little waterway called Musquatch Brook, this cove is host to more development and overall human clutter than its southeastern counterpart. The scene offers an enigmatic contrast: the old, in the form of the disintegrating remains of the turn-of-the-century boardwalk, and the new, the bustling Shark River Hills Marina, one of the busiest on the estuary. The 585-foot boardwalk once served as the promenade of the regal Hotel Van Dyke, built in the late 1870s and destroyed by fire early in this century. In its bright but rather brief heyday the hotel served as the scene of fun and frolic for the well-to-do.*

imported plume grass, a picturesque exotic plant that looks good but which provides little in the way of food for wildlife.

To locate a "special" square mile in New Jersey, a unique little tract that offers something of the best and the brightest right along with the people aspect of the Garden State, one must, I think, look to one of the state's greatest assets, the edge of the sea. It is estimated that by the year 2010, 75 percent of the population of the United States will live within fifty miles of the seacoasts. The effect of this population growth on the marine and littoral environment will be profound and considerable. The Jersey shore's human population has grown tremendously over the past twenty years, so that today the impact of that growth on the coastal environment is at once considerable as well as visually and audibly evident.

Take Monmouth County's Shark River Inlet and estuary, for example. In totality not much greater than a square mile in area, this boat anchorage and sheltered harbor is one of the most popular and busiest on the Middle Atlantic seacoast. Only a little more than an hour's drive from the New York metropolitan area, it is home to the state's largest charter and party boat fleet and numerous private craft, berthed at five busy marinas. Three highway drawbridges and one railroad crossing span the inlet's deep channel, the busiest, the Route 35 bridge, rising to allow the passage of boats some six thousand times a year. During the busier summer weekends, as many as one hundred thousand fun seekers crowd the streets and boardwalks of the nearby shore towns of Avon-by-the-Sea and Belmar. A modest but growing lobster and eel fishing fleet is based here, and during the warmer months a sizable flotilla of motorboats, kayaks, sailboats, and jetskis plies the broad

Pigeons foraging on the beach.

Pigeons at the beach. *Among all the many and varied beach scavengers, the rock dove, or "street pigeon," is one of the most numerous, especially in the vicinity of the larger shore towns. These birds patrol the ocean and estuary beaches with a diligence matched only by those consummate marine opportunists, the gulls, and little is missed among the tangle of sea wrack. Interestingly enough, when on the beach, pigeons are somewhat more wary than when strutting amiably about town and city streets and will not allow the familiarity they do "in town." This group inspected and pecked at objects of interest with apparent nonchalance, but when I shifted a bit, two of them watched me with growing apprehension, in the wide-eyed, vaguely dopey way of pigeons everywhere; when the page I was working on lifted suddenly in the sea breeze, they all flapped noisily off.*

Nearby, another, much less common beach gleaner was at work repairing its "digs" above the high-tide line. The ghost crab is a true terrestrial crab in that, as an adult, it never enters the water unless forced to; it will drown if forcibly submerged. This creature is a common inhabitant of wide sand beaches from New Jersey to the Gulf of Mexico, though it is far more common in the southern part of the range. On the busy beaches just outside Shark River Inlet, a small number of these crabs hang on, virtually unknown to sun worshipers for they are strongly nocturnal in nature. During the day, the only evidence of their presence is the openings of their burrows—about as wide as a fifty-cent piece for the adult crab—that dot the upper beach among scattered clumps of dune grass. An intricate network of tiny tracks radiating outward from the burrow are the sole indication that the hole is home to something. The crabs nervously pop up and down, energetically shoving out excess sand and otherwise repairing their burrows as often as they can without being stepped on. At night, the picture changes, and the beach walker carrying a strong flashlight will be rewarded by the sight of a multitude of pale whitish little imps scuttling swiftly over the dark sands, their eyes reflecting bright green eyeshine.

Tunnels of another kind will be found in pilings and driftwood. These intricate borings are the work of the shipworm, commonly known as the "gribble." The gribble is the ancient enemy of mariners, having caused great structural damage to piers and wood-hulled boats over the centuries. Pressure-treated or creosote-impregnated wood discourages them for a time, but as the wood ages, the gribbles move in and set up shop. This scrap of wood was found on the upper beach among the ghost crab burrows, and in addition to drawing it, I took it home as an attractive example of "beach art."

Shipworm damage.

Street pigeons. *I watched these on the sun-washed boards of the empty public fishing pier at the Belmar Marina. In this drawing I have to admit that I was thinking "arty," pondering the stark yet attractive contrast between the soft, rounded forms of the birds and the heavy, dark, and angular construction of the weathered dock. The rather strong breeze was out of the northwest, and all the birds but one, this one crouched beside a rail stanchion, were facing into it.*

expanse of the estuary. Overall, Shark River, like New Jersey as a whole, is highly popular with people.

What special attributes, then, would make a square mile of the Shark River environment worth recording in line and prose? To find the answer to that question, one must look to the nearby ocean itself. New Jersey's first human residents maintained very close ties to the seacoast. In pre-European times the Shark River environs were occupied by the Matawan Indians, one of the tribes of the Unami, a major division of the Lenni Lenape ("original") peoples. To the early residents, the peninsula that would one day become the state of New Jersey was *Scheyechbi*—"the land along the water"—and during the warmer months of the year the original Americans gravitated to the richly endowed, and for the most part benign, coastal environment to fish and harvest the abundant clams and oysters of the estuaries and sounds. Droves of harried urbanites do likewise via the Garden

A trawler surrounded by gulls. *Trawlers are a common sight just offshore in the fall and winter months. For the most part, they are catching and processing bottom fish, such as flounder, whiting, and sea bass, though some coastal draggers are specially geared up to harvest surf clams for the chowder and canning industries. This boat, which I drew shortly after dawn on a calm, flat sea, was not under way and because the penetrating roar of diesels reached my shore-based ears and the air above the craft was full of hopeful gulls, I speculated that the crew was in the process of sorting the catch, tossing the rejects to the waiting birds and icing down the remainder.*

State Parkway today, though the tasty bivalves are not the object of this modern pilgrimage. The oysters are all but gone from the bays, and today a visitor would eat a clam fresh from a Shark River mudflat at his or her peril.

In the seventeenth century Shark River was a very different sort of place than it is today. For one thing, its broad estuary didn't exist then; it was dredged over many decades, beginning in the mid-1800s, with the present configuration gradually taking shape in

the 1920s. In the 1800s, the Indians knew the river, then "very swift and deep and over 100 yards in breadth," as *Nolletquesset.* The clear, clean stream emptied into the sea between two tiny, rustic fishing hamlets called Ocean Beach and Key East—the present-day shore towns of Belmar and Avon-by-the-Sea.

To the early English settlers, the stream was known as the Hogs Pond River because of the extensive pig farms

White pine on dune. *A young white pine lends its feathery grace to a rather unlikely environment for a forest tree—a windswept dune at the beachfront. It's hard to say whether this tree was the result of a deliberate planting to help stabilize the dune or whether it arrived via windblown seed. In any case, such scattered conifers offer welcome shelter to yellow-rumped warblers that frequent the beaches and to the occasional saw-whet owl.*

Heavy surf. *It can be difficult to express the power of wind and wave at the edge of the sea. Visiting the inlet mouth early one morning, I was struck by the chaotic yet somehow rhythmic motion going on all at once: the ragged, wind-driven clouds, the choppy, pewter-gray sea, the wind-whipped grasses, the pounding surf at the jetty's end, and the lone angler and crowd of grounded gulls leaning into the wind's raw power. A light but penetrating rain filled the air, so I made this drawing from inside my rocking and rolling van.*

then sprawled along its sylvan banks, and according to local legend the present name was adopted in the early 1800s after a large shark was reportedly swept upriver by the incoming tide and perished in the fresh waters of Hogs Pond. It was really no more dramatic than that.

Once the river had been dredged and opened to commercial and recreational boat traffic, it displayed, unlike many East Coast inlets, a remarkable staying power; only once, in 1877, was Shark River inlet closed to navigation completely. A sandbar sealed off the entrance during a fierce storm in August of that year, and it took hundreds of volunteers four days and nights to clear it. The inlet was widened and dredged again in 1881, and since then, although the persistent bar still shifts and moves about according to the whim of the winds and tides, it has not seriously threatened egress to Shark River's snug anchorage.

The estuarine environment as an ecological entity, anywhere in the world, has finally come to be recognized for the incredibly diverse, biologically rich living system that it is. And although the Shark River estuary is situated in a long-established suburban setting and heavily utilized by people virtually year-round, the renewing and cleansing power of the sea has helped ensure that, with few exceptions, its

Blue mussels and three large frilled anemones sharing a foothold in a sheltered jetty tidepool. *The size and number of anemones are usually governed by the degree of protection from the surf and powerful currents that a particular jetty nook offers. These animals were anchored to a rock well recessed in a pool on the north side of the inlet jetty, the place seldom battered by heavy waves, even at higher tides. Getting to the spot involved literally crawling on all fours with my sketch pad in my teeth over rocks coated with algae that looked and felt like wet spinach and noodles. The water was a reasonable sixty-nine degrees Fahrenheit, so the required ten-minute squat in the lapping waves while I captured the creatures on paper wasn't the ordeal it likely would have been a month later.*

still-rich biodiversity will likely enter the third millennium reasonably intact.

The square mile that encompasses Shark River estuary, from the shorefront inlet west to the point of mergence of the fresh waters of the river with the tidal influence of this small bay, presents the observer with four distinct and unique habitats. In an east-to-west progression, they are: the oceanfront littoral; the tidal bay; the salt marsh; and the riverine lowland forest. Although the character of this coastal river system prior to the coming of Europeans was pristine and untrammeled in the classic sense of the word, there is no doubt that all four of

these ecosystems were, at least in part, created by humans and have undergone a tremendous change, owing to considerable and repeated manipulation and alteration over the past three centuries. But in spite of this irreversible fact, there is much life here, carried in daily by the push of the incoming tide and removed six hours later by its ebb. Coursing through the inlet and the deep channel—which also conveys the people of this place in their travels and in their commerce—all enter the estuary in a great and ponderous silence, this amazing collection of wondrous, vibrant life, in all its colors and shapes and sizes and stages of

Cormorants. *I thought this crowd of double-crested cormorants on the free-standing pilings of a dismantled pier presented an interesting study of spare angles and the restless sea. It was a windy, bright day at the beach, and a strong swell was running, causing the now dock-less uprights to sway languidly with each incoming roller. The giddy motion seemed not to affect the birds in the least; they preened, squabbled, and jostled for space like a bunch of kids on a cafeteria line.*

hour of every day of every year, in the endless cycle of the sea.

The Shark River estuary, thus, is an integral part of the works and happenings of the people that surround it, crowd in upon it, give it its unique "Jersey shore" flavor, and in many ways define its very geographical boundaries. Yet it is also very much a world apart, a place, where—in spite of the many indignities and controls that people have placed upon it, no matter the bridges that span, and the bulkheads that contain, its waters—the life processes move with an irresistible will, a glacierlike momentum that will be brought to a halt only when the planet itself is rendered completely uninhabitable for all its inhabitants.

And in that respect, this one small piece of the world, this one square mile, where people and their environment come together in a pleasant, sometimes frenetic, often heavy-handed love affair, yet a very tenuous arrangement, is as apropos of New Jersey as any of the state's remaining eight thousand-plus square miles. It is a place where people work and play and spin out their lives virtually astride a hidden aquatic world of wonderful variety and literally brimming with life. It is a place highly popular with all of its myriad inhabitants, from human sun worshipers to summer flounders, from shore commuters to crab dippers, from gulls

development. And here it is held and nurtured for its allotted time and spins out its destiny before returning to that physical mother of all life on earth. All this change and life and death occur, mostly unseen by human eyes, at every

The Ocean Avenue drawbridge. *This is the first of three crossings the incoming boat must pass beneath on the way into the harbor. During the off-season, when both vehicular and boat traffic are at a minimum, the raising of the bridge causes little inconvenience to motorists, but during the busy summer months, it's another story altogether.*

This drawing of the bridge was executed in a two-step procedure that allowed me to render a relatively detailed drawing of both the stationary structure and the passing boat. I positioned myself at a desirable vantage point at about 4:30 P.M., when the charter and party boat fleet normally returns to port for the day. With at least a dozen craft passing through the channel, I knew that the bridge would be raised for at least fifteen minutes, giving me plenty of time to sketch it in that position. The boat was a bit trickier. As the Big Marie SII, one of the largest of the harbor's party boats, went under the span, I very quickly and roughly sketched her and the wave action, and then later drove to her berth at the marina where I filled in the structural details at leisure.

and grubbies to girl watchers, weekend mariners, and kids casting for snappers. My square mile of Shark River does not pretend to offer the reader a glimpse of unsullied nature—perhaps one must journey to the Antarctic or Greenland for that—but rather an environment that has felt and continues to feel the presence of humans, and yet manages to cleanse and renew itself in the six-hour cycle of the eternal tides. In my view, this little estuary, this one small square mile among all the millions that comprise the planet Earth, holds the eminent right of environmental survivorship.

And in that respect, Shark River, in both its vibrant and diverse past and present, as well as its hopeful future, is very much the best of New Jersey and typifies the essence of the Atlantic Coast.

Part I

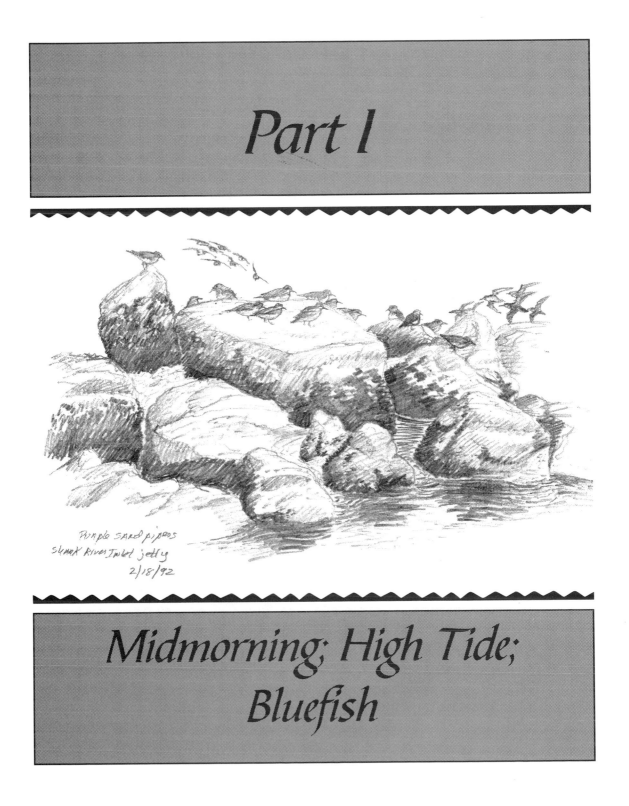

Purple Sandpipers
Shark River Inlet jetty
2/18/92

Midmorning; High Tide;
Bluefish

In the detail sketch labels (handwritten):
prominent electrical organs on fishe's head
detail of head and mouth, from above

Stargazer. *This composite drawing illustrates one of those field opportunities that doesn't come along every day of the week. The bizarre stargazer* (Astroscopus guttatus) *is not an overly rare marine fish, but being a secretive, nocturnal sand burrower, it is seldom seen—unless it comes to grief on the beach, as this one did. I came across this fourteen-inch specimen lying on the oceanfront beach on a windy April morning. It was being picked over by a juvenile black-backed gull, which reluctantly abandoned its prize with clearly expressed resentment (I was the bigger scavenger, so I won); the fish was quite fresh, and, incredibly, the body twitched and flexed reflexively for nearly an hour afterward even though the hapless creature's internal viscera had been plucked and devoured by the gull!*

The stargazer shares with the famous electric eel the ability to generate enough juice to numb hand or foot if a large one is picked up by the head or stepped on while wading. The prominent, triangular electrical organs may be seen in the detail sketch of the head. This particular stargazer was retained as a biological specimen because of its large size and fully adult color and pattern; it was photographed and then preserved in formalin by an ichthyologist friend.

When the boat traveler enters the Shark River estuary from the channel, the first impression is very much that of a modest-sized freshwater lake. Under the influence of all but the foulest weather, the estuary, less than two miles square in its entire water surface area, has the placid appearance of a millpond. The angry chop of storms and the attendant whitecaps are a rather uncommon sight here, for this is a well-protected anchorage, shielded from the sea and the northeast winds by a half-mile of former dunes long ago rendered into suburbia. It is only when the winds direct their assault from the southeast, giving it the entire, broad south arm of the bay through which to "breeze up," that the river reveals its tie to the ocean and its many moods.

But moving over the little bay's riffled surface, surrounded on all sides by its remnant marshes and wooded shores, the latter well populated with human constructions, one has only to look down to get a true sense of place. Dip a finger in the passing flow; it is very much salt, nearly as briny as the trackless waters above the sunken canyons far offshore. And no jellyfish or flitting, fiercely predatory arrow worms or insatiable bluefish ever plied the

A piping plover. *I drew this lone bird as it poised daintily at the surf's verge in the soft light of dawn, and I had the odd feeling that it might well be the last of its species I, personally, might ever see. Twenty-five years ago this delightful little "sand peep" was quite common on the barrier beaches of New Jersey; I recall seeing at least a dozen pairs breeding on the then-empty beaches of Brigantine Island and the wonderful experience of holding one of the tiny, innocent chicks in the palm of my hand. Today the plover is restricted to very small colonies in a few rigidly protected spots along the coast: a few pairs breed at heavily peopled Sandy Hook (incredibly enough) as well as at the Holgate section of Brigantine Wildlife Refuge near Atlantic City; elsewhere, the species has simply been pushed out by increasingly heavy human utilization of the beachfront for development and summer recreation. The piping plover is federally classed as Endangered throughout its range.*

Sea foam. *A gray, misty morning with big surf running produced "sea foam" of questionable composition on the Belmar beach. In the surf, the stuff had the fluffy, pure-white look of soapsuds and appeared almost beautiful as it roiled and swirled like swashing whipped cream. Higher on the beach, above the tide line, it turned a curious, pale tannish color, and sections of it separated from the lumpy windrows and blew off across the deserted strand like big, sudsy tumbleweeds. I cautiously plucked up a handful of the stuff; it was odorless and disintegrated quickly in my hand. Maybe it was a natural product of the sea, or . . .*

gentle depths of an inland lake; these are true creatures of the great oceans, brought here, deep within the enclosing arms of the estuary, by the timeless run and flow of the tides.

Make no mistake about it, civilized and cluttered though the land-based surroundings may be, when you set sail upon Shark River or dive beneath its waves and the noisy wakes of boats, you are at sea.

Most of the creatures of the deep have their origins here, in the world of the estuary. Here is the pulse of life, of the very planet itself. Within the containment of the estuary, the saline lifeblood of the earth slips in through the atrium of the channel, bringing with it the bounty from without, from the abyss.

To find the aquatic tapestry of life in all its wonderful profusion and variety, one must visit the *edge* of the sea, that special place where sea meets dry land. To look for life in all its many stages, colors, and manifestations, one can hardly do better than to discover and observe the secrets of the littoral, the nutrient-rich expanses of the estuary.

Yellow wrack, or bladder wrack. *A common brown alga of the lower intertidal zone, this forms dense colonies on jetty rocks and dock pilings.*

Young laughing gulls. *In mid-September large numbers of young-of-the-year laughing gulls gather on the beaches and mudflats of Shark River in preparation for the move south. Given the garrulous nature of their parents earlier in the year, these young birds are oddly silent, simply assembling in low-keyed groups that patrol the beaches for food items and spend a lot of time at personal toilet. Their behavior has the feel of expectancy to it.*

Young laughing gull. *Here, I focused on one bird out of many and simply observed and recorded its many poses. The laughing gull is without a doubt the most attractive of the local gulls, with its trim, dovelike form, inquisitive nature, and striking breeding colors.*

Terns. *The membership of this little gathering was constantly changing as individuals came and went, mostly on fishing forays above the nearby surf. The birds were not diving for fishes, but rather making light, dipping, shallow dives in which they plucked some small prey from the surface of the water. I suspected they were after spawning mysid shrimp, which swarm at the water's surface in vast numbers in May.*

The tide is at the core of an estuary's undefinable character. It has its patient way with the land, slipping silently in from the deeps and covering it yet again, and then rearranging and shifting it about, albeit in minute but clearly discernible ways. A human footprint or a tire track may endure for decades on the treeless, seemingly timeless tundra, but all sign of a tread, barefoot or shod, will be erased within minutes on a coastal mudflat welcoming the new tide. Instituted by distant, cosmic forces, nudged along by gentle zephyrs, running and rilling inexorably over mud, sand, and stone, creeping up jetty

rocks and pilings, lifting grounded boats, bringing in new life from the sea, the tide is irresistible.

City sparrows at the beach. *The narrow, ever-changing environment where the sea meets the land is a virtual repository of edibles—if you know where and how to look for them. The beach, whether at the oceanfront or along the protected estuary shoreline, is the haunt of scavengers, and sometimes these take on a rather surprising character. One would expect the ubiquitous gulls to materialize out of nowhere at the first hint of a handout. But house sparrows as "beach birds"? The house sparrow, a.k.a. the "English sparrow," can work the beach as expertly and effectively as any gull or sandpiper. Alert, enterprising, and aggressive, a flock of "chippies" patrolling the wrack line doesn't miss much. These birds will eat anything from beach fleas and sand hoppers (both isopods), through fish and horseshoe crab eggs, to organic human trash. They are exceeded in number on the strand only by gulls, and possibly by starlings and street pigeons.*

House sparrows are, as any suburbanite or city dweller knows, quite fearless; these birds allowed a very close approach while I sketched them with a Wolff HB carbon pencil.

detail of eye

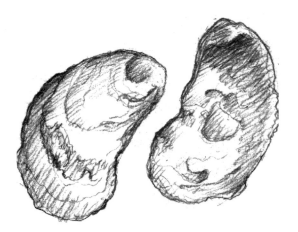

Creatures in jeopardy. *These drawings show two animals that have suffered a considerable decline, the horseshoe crab, owing to direct persecution, and the oyster, the victim of pollution of coastal waters. The horseshoe has existed as we know it today for more than 250 million years; it is a true "living fossil" in that it has no living relatives, and ancestral forms*

found in the fossil record are virtually identical to it. This formidable-looking but completely harmless creature was once abundant throughout its range, which extends from southern New England to Yucatan. In the past it was used extensively for fertilizer, and today it is collected locally and used as bait for lobster and eel traps. In Shark River, a renewed lobster and eel pot fishery has resulted in the gradual disappearance of these fascinating animals over the past five years; at this time, horseshoes are not afforded protection by law, and thus their harvesting is not controlled or regulated in any way.

The oyster has experienced a similar decline in Shark River, which was once the site of a very active fishery. Increased development of the surrounding area and the resultant street and sewer runoff have resulted in the estuary's bivalve fisheries (clams, mussels, and oysters) being periodically but regularly closed both to commercial and recreational diggers. This particular shell was large, nearly five inches, indicating that a few healthy beds still exist in the deeper channels and rocky areas of the estuary.

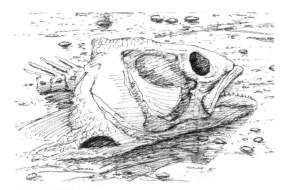

The bluefish (Pomatomus saltatrix). *Attaining the maximum length of about three feet and weights of up to twenty-four pounds, the adult blue is a formidable marine predator, well able to wreak havoc among the vast schools of herring, mackerel, and smaller "bait fish" species, and large individuals have been implicated in "attacks" on human bathers on the New England coast. In these incidents, always carried out by larger, school blues, the human victims are simply in the way when the big fish are avidly chasing prey fishes close inshore and attacking them in a wild melee.*

The desiccated bluefish head shown in the field sketch, that of a large school, or "chopper blue," did not meet its end because of natural causes and drift ashore, but rather is the remains of a fish cleaned by a successful angler at a nearby marina. Contrary to marine regulations, many heads and "racks," or stripped backbones, are simply tossed into the water at docks. These eventually drift ashore and provide abundant provender for scavengers. This severed head, though in an advanced state of decay, clearly shows the powerful jaw structure and capable teeth of this legendary aquatic eating machine.

Goldenrod and terns. *These large, rather ancient clumps of seaside goldenrod have persisted on the beach at the mouth of the inlet for many years, in spite of heavy human foot traffic during the summer months. This hardy plant is another of the "front line" terrestrial flora of the littoral zone, taking root as close to the ocean as the vagaries of weather and the ever-shifting dunes permit. Once established, the root systems run deep into the sand and serve as an anchor, allowing the plant to survive all manner of environmental efforts to dislodge it.*

On the day I drew the sketch, this spot was alive with a noisy, active flock of little least terns, one of the more delightful of the summer "beach birds." Although the "leasties" no longer nest on this section of beach owing to the overwhelming human presence during the summer, there are active colonies farther south in the Holgate section of Brigantine National Wildlife Refuge.

Least terns are quite relaxed and fearless (when away from the nesting grounds) and will permit a fairly close approach. I sketched these three individuals from a distance of about twenty feet with a Wolff's HB carbon pencil.

Gr. Black-backed gulls.
8/7/91
I'm not sure what this
wharf once was—probably an
ancient pier.

Cormorants. *During the month of August, the resident cormorants seem to become more restless and prone to wanderlust than usual, and many are seen winging their way up and down the coast in search of offshore fishing grounds. Cormorants (the common name is a corruption of the Latin,* corvus, *or* "crow," *and* marinus, *or* "sea") *are often mistaken for geese by inexperienced birders, but they can be told from the latter by their solid black color, their habit of holding the head above the horizontal when in flight, and their large flocks strung out just above the water's surface in long, undulating lines.*

I was leisurely sketching the incoming tide burbling in and around the rocks at "land's end" when a flock of these "sea crows" rambled by in a long, undulating line offshore, heading north. It was an easy matter to jot them in, almost as an afterthought to the drawing, in yet another of the many surprises that may await the artist who happens to be in the right place at the right time.

Black-backed gulls. *On the Jersey shore, the dog days of the eighth month of the year are characterized by hazy, China-blue skies and a flat, gently rolling sea. At times, except for the ever-plunging surf, virtually nothing moves along the blazing beaches save for the occasional languid shifting of a well-bronzed sun worshiper and a gull or two picking over the sea wrack. There are also scenes of muted yet striking visual contrast. Not far from the inlet there stands the very last vestige of a once popular fishing pier. At one time, this structure extended hundreds of feet into the ocean; today it is a sun-bleached, wave-battered derelict.*

I happened along on such a bright, windless day, and perching on the jetty rocks nearby, I unlimbered my pen and proceeded to rough in the basic form of the weathered wood. As the sketch neared completion, a big black-backed gull sailed in and alighted on the seaward piling; it was soon joined by two more, and since these powerful, impressive birds gave every indication that they intended to hang around for a while, I quickly added them to the drawing. This was just one of those little surprises that make field sketching the enjoyable experience it is!

slips back and away from the land; a mere slip of receding, opaque film, it seems somehow drained of its life-load, devoid of activity and fish life. It has a roiled and muddy look and leaves all manner of minute debris and the usual collection of natural and man-made flotsam and jetsam in its wake.

On the rising tide, the water has a

Ubiquitous sights. *For some reason, ordinary snow fencing seems to appeal to the sense of the aesthetic in artists and photographers, for its stark, spare lines and rickety constructions often figure prominently in paintings and photos of shoreside locales. On the Belmar beach at Shark River Inlet, the fencing has two functions: it inhibits sand movement to some degree, and, perhaps more important, it serves as a litter catchall, preventing the trash discarded by thoughtless beachgoers from blowing into the roadways or into the channel itself.*

Starlings, among the most persistent and efficient of the oceanfront's avian cleanup crews, are virtually everywhere during the busy summer season, strutting about on the beaches, panhandling food scraps on the boardwalk, or clambering around inside overstuffed trash containers in search of fast-food edibles.

At Shark River I've witnessed the daily arrival of the tide primarily by observing the actions of the fishes at its advancing, tentative lip. On the ebb, the thinning sheet of water reluctantly

Plovers. *In mid-August, the first of the little "wind birds," or semipalmated plovers, make their appearance along the beaches as they move south along the coast toward their subtropical wintering grounds. This drawing was completed in two stages; I was intrigued by the composition and form offered by the ancient pilings poking up from the wet sand and surf and was in the process of rendering that subject alone, when the little flock of plovers skimmed in out of nowhere and obligingly alighted at front-and-center stage. They immediately set about probing the wave-washed sand for isopods and other tiny marine life.*

fresh, bottle-green clarity to it, slipping over the land with an investigative, almost aggressive air. The incoming tide is loaded with promise, and all the myriad creatures dependent on it for life seem to sense this. In summer multitudes of tiny fishes eagerly press up the gently shelving flats and beaches at its very vanguard, scouring and exploring every nook and crevice of the dry land as it reenters their domain for the first time in six hours. At a depth of a few mere millimeters, at the very point where the continent meets the sea, the intense struggle for survival goes on.

On the Atlantic Coast, high and low tides are experienced on average about six hours and thirteen minutes apart, meaning that successive high tides will occur roughly twelve hours and twenty-six minutes apart. The schedule for high and low tides advances by about fifty-five minutes each successive day.

The gravitational pull of the moon accounts for between 66 and 80 percent of the normal tide activity, that of the sun provides the remainder. The extent of tidal rise and fall can vary from a few inches, as in the wide and shallow Barnegat Bay or Chesapeake Bay, to more than forty feet in Nova Scotia's deep, narrow Bay of Fundy; at Shark River, the average distance between the mean low- and high-tide marks is about eighteen inches, a modest fluctuation,

to be sure, but one that exposes an astonishing expanse of the bay to the air each day. The highest tides occur when the earth, sun, and moon are in apogee, or direct alignment with one another. This occurs twice each lunar month (of twenty-eight and a half days) with the new and full moons.

Shark River is a typical East Coast estuary in that the saline sea pours in through a narrow inlet and channel and spreads out into the small bay, where it meets the descending fresh waters of the river flowing east toward the ocean. What happens when these two great aquatic entities come together is not the simple and homogeneous mixing of fresh and salt water in the manner one might expect, but rather an interesting phenomenon called the "wedge effect." It's a variation on the old theme "oil and water don't mix."

Salt water is much denser and thus heavier than fresh, and when the incoming tide meets the flow of the river's discharge, the two masses of water tend to form two complementary wedges—the heavier salt below, the fresh water above. Salinity is measured in parts per thousand (ppt); that is, the sea a mile or so off Shark River Inlet will have the concentration of about thirty-five ppt, or about thirty-five grams of dissolved solids in 1,000 grams of water. Closer to the inlet's mouth that reading may be between thirty and

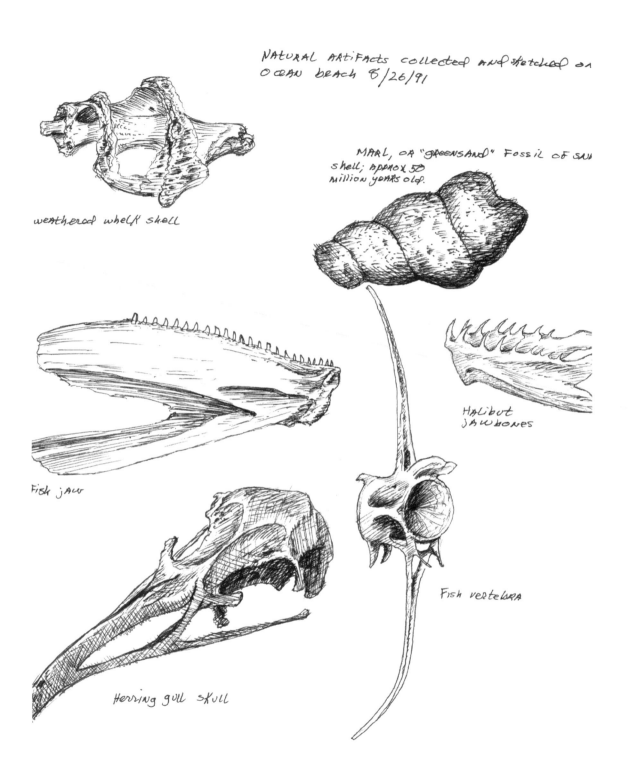

NATURAL ARTIFACTS collected AND sketched on OCEAN beach 8/26/91

weathered whelk shell

MARL, OR "GREENSAND" FOSSIL OF SNAIL shell; APPROX 50 million years old.

Fish jaw

HALIBUT JAWBONES

Fish vertebra

Herring gull skull

Gifts from the hurricane. *In the wake of any powerful coastal storm, a treasure trove of natural artifacts are ferreted from their submarine hiding places by the action of wind and wave and deposited on the shore for the beachcomber's pleasure. Most of those shown in this drawing are rather "everyday" objects of the coastal environment, but one, found among the rocks of an oceanfront groin shortly after the tumultuous visit of Hurricane Bob, proved to be of a bit more interest.*

At first, I was sure the object was some sort of sculpture of human, and recent, origin, so regular and geometric was its design. Composed of the green marl, or "greensand," commonly found on New Jersey beaches, it had spiral indentations that looked so sharp as to have been deliberately carved in the soft stone. A check with John Maisey, a paleontologist at New York's American Museum of Natural History, revealed that the object was in fact the fossilized greensand remains of an ancient snail, approximately forty million years of age.

thirty-two ppt, while at the mouth of the river it may be as low as five to seven ppt—much too low to support such strictly marine organisms as starfish and sea urchins.

Under ideal conditions, that is, with little wind or boat traffic, the dual levels of salt and fresh water can coexist for some time and over a broad area of the estuary. In the tidal creeks, clams and mussels may thrive on the bottom in a strictly saline environment, while a few feet above, at the surface, the water may be fresh enough to drink. Likewise, frogs (which cannot tolerate a saline environment) and many species of inland, freshwater fishes have been known to penetrate far into coastal estuaries when conditions are right.

But at Shark River, the mix of waters occurs more quickly and completely under the physical conditions usually extant here. The boat channels are many and deep and well traveled, and the shoreline is studded with a plethora of manmade structures, such as docks, bulkheads, and scattered sunken wrecks that interrupt and disperse the natural flow. In a sense, the character of this estuary constitutes a "mechanical mixing" of sorts, the only method by which to effect the swift and homogeneous blending of any two fluids. In midsummer boat traffic is heavy and nearly continuous, so that a fully brackish situation exists well into the mouth of the river itself.

In any estuary, the power and mystery of the tides are the harbingers of many natural events great and small. Shark River at dead low tide has the look, not to mention the effervescence, of a pond suddenly and nearly completely drained of its water, but it is then a place of much more activity and sound than when the incoming sea has reached the berm or upper beach, for a virtual army of birds, from the very

The north-facing side of the Shark River Inlet jetty. *The jetty lies in the lee of the prevailing coastal winds and thus affords the beach there greater protection from wave erosion. Because the heaviest surf is generally fended off here, the rocks below the midlittoral zone are literally carpeted with life, in particular, matted masses of blue mussels. Looking at this scene one morning, I was struck by the sharply defined contrast in textures: the nubby, ruglike texture of the mussels yielding higher up to the flat, weather-worn planes of the exposed rock surfaces.*

In this drawing I decided to use a round-tipped permanent marker to rough in the broad areas of dark shadows and define the basic bulk of the jetty. The fine-line pen was then brought into play to produce the linear effect of the upper rock surfaces, and using a quick, circular "curlicue" stroke, I could easily achieve the rough-textured look of the mussel beds.

Rendering such a transient natural "object" as a breaking wave is not as difficult as it might seem to be. On a relatively windless day with a fairly regular and "easy" surf coming in, each succeeding wave strikes the shore and breaks upon the rocks with essentially the same configuration of water action and spray. It's thus a simple matter to continue sketching in the details of perhaps ten successive waves into your single image until your drawing is literally a composite, but very believable, roller.

Ghost crabs. *This stretch of ocean beach is designated as "fishing only" and off-limits to bathers; thus a colony of those little beach waifs, the ghost crabs, have set up housekeeping without much danger of being trampled on by humans.*

The small colony near Shark River is somewhat unusual and very much tenuous in nature, for the animal is rare north of Virginia. These particular crabs were extremely furtive and quite skittish and wary. I managed to secure this drawing of one by sitting motionless about ten feet from a burrow until an individual cautiously emerged after about fifteen minutes to have a look around. It reacted every time my pen moved upon the page but remained in sight (though closely hugging the safety of its burrow) long enough for me to secure a good study. I sketched this bustling colony on September 18. That night a cold front moved through the area, and the following day—a brisk and windy one—neither crab nor burrow was to be seen.

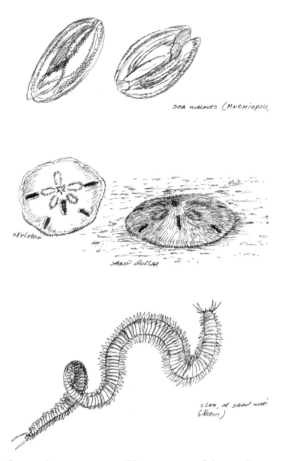

sea walnuts (Mnemiopsis)

skeleton

sand dollar

clam, or sandworm
(Nereis)

More small aquatic creatures of the estuarine environment. Upper figures: *both the green sea slug and the striped nudibranch are common animals in the summer shallows, being found in some abundance in the dense eelgrass and widgeon grass beds. I've attempted to keep them in aquaria but with little luck.* Lower figures: *several species of anthozoans, or sea anemones, occupy any and all rocks, bulkheads, and pilings throughout the eastern part of the estuary, where the salinity undergoes less tidal fluctuation. The commonest and largest species is* Metridium senile, *the frilled anemone; fully adult individuals may reach six inches in height and measure four inches across the base, or column. They are a most attractive brick-red color with white or cream-colored tentacles and will thrive in the balanced marine aquarium if adequately fed. All the creatures pictured here were collected and removed from the environment (the anemones with a piece of their attachment substrate) and placed in a two-gallon aquarium for the posing session.*

Invertebrate portraits. *Here are some of the smaller invertebrate life of Shark River.* Upper: *sea walnuts, common ctenophores closely related to jellyfish.* Center: *sand dollars, close relatives of the familiar sea urchins; these creatures are seldom seen alive by beachcombers, but the sun-dried skeletons often turn up on the beaches.* Bottom: *the clam, or sandworm, a highly popular flounder bait all along the Atlantic coast.*

green sea slug

Black-backed gull. *In the soft, new light of the morning, a great black-backed gull arranges its plumage on a channel marker buoy.*

Rats! *Inveterate and dedicated anglers, especially those seeking the noble striped bass, are often referred to locally as "jetty rats" simply because they always seem to be out there and to know every rock and riptide around "the rocks." But as this sketch shows, there are plenty of the real thing in residence on every jetty and groin on the coast.*

The all-too-common Norway rat is the one single mammalian species—and a terrestrial one at that—to be found living with perfect contentment among the jumbled rocks of jetties and groins, functioning as both predator and scavenger. I was presented with rather dramatic evidence of this recently while fishing a jetty during a rising, full-moon tide. Positioned about halfway out the jetty's length, I chanced to glance seaward as the tide neared full high, the rollers beginning to thunder and wash over the upper rocks. Near the jetty's seaward end, I suddenly spotted a number of strange "little brown things" fitfully hopping up and down, but evidently moving toward me. Very shortly I saw that they were rats, big ones, apparently trying to escape the rapidly rising water by fleeing up and down over the rocks toward the beach; I realized I was directly in their path. The sight of the rapidly advancing rats, jumping from rock to rock, very much put the idea of flight into my own head, but since the jetty was fairly wide, I opted to stay put and wait out events. The wet, bedraggled creatures—six of them, it turned out— came abreast of me and passed within a few feet. One paused and looked up at me with its bright, black eyes, as if to say, "Gimme a break, I've got troubles enough." So I stood aside and watched them scamper out of sight, to the safety of dry land.

Starfish, or seastars. *These are most cooperative sketch subjects for their degree of activity is not what one could call hyper! I caught this duo investigating a bed of blue mussels at extreme low tide on the inlet's channel. Starfish, plodding and inactive though they may appear, are the chief and deadliest predator of mussels and oysters and devour thousands of them. These familiar echnoderms ("spiny skin") are often fabulously abundant in the shallow water of the channel during the warmer months, withdrawing offshore in late fall.*

terrestrial avian opportunists like starlings, crows, and pigeons to the species characteristic of the littoral, fan out over the emerging flats and partake of the banquet spread there. Insistent, strident, such low-tide pandemonium among the birds carries the suggestion of urgency—and indeed it is urgent— for the bounteous table of the mudflats is not spread for terrestrial inspection and dining for very long. Soon, the tide will turn, and the incoming waters of the sea will prevail once more, transporting this unique, peculiar land of sea and sky and sand back into the aquatic half of its personality.

The incoming tide bears many gifts from the sea, not the least of them the scrappy, snappy, magnificent bluefish. Alternately scorned and revered by sport fishermen, *Pomatomus saltatrix* has

Seaside goldenrod in full bloom. *In early October this hardy coastal plant puts on its best and brightest floral display. The tawny, windswept beaches, otherwise bereft of most of summer's faded flowers, are now graced by the stately plants, with their rich green leaves and vibrant yellow plumes. The blooming of the adventurous "weed" is a vivid illustration of the fact that if a vacuum exists anywhere in nature, an organism moves to fill it.*

spotted sandpipers
on jetty rocks.
10/4/91

The ultimate fate of wood and steel perched at the very edge of the continent. *Once the anchor for the jetty and secured within a flanking of one-ton boulders, the gridwork and pilings have been exposed by the inexorable poundings of the breaking surf and now lie exposed to the full force of the elements. The cumulative power of the sea can be seen in the two outer steel uprights, bent at angles as by the hand of a giant as the now-vanished upper beam was torn loose during a past nor'easter.*

A young laughing gull under the noonday sun at high tide.

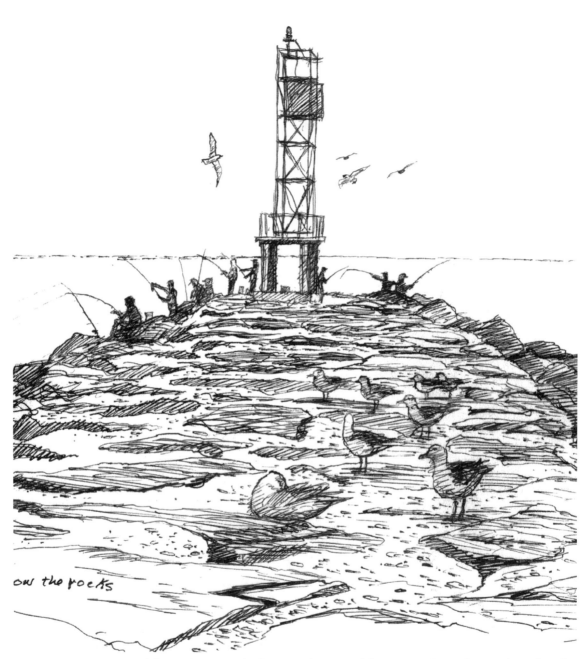

on the rocks

A busy day at the jetty. *The south jetty at Shark River Inlet is one of the most popular in the state, being broad and flat and thus easily traversed. It is never submerged, even at the highest tides, and thus the rocks are usually dry and free of the slippery algae that make some of the other "rocks" up and down the coast a challenge to navigate, especially at night. Most experienced anglers, especially those seeking striped bass, use cleated boots or strap-ons called "rock walkers" in order to maintain footing on the trickier groins and jetties.*

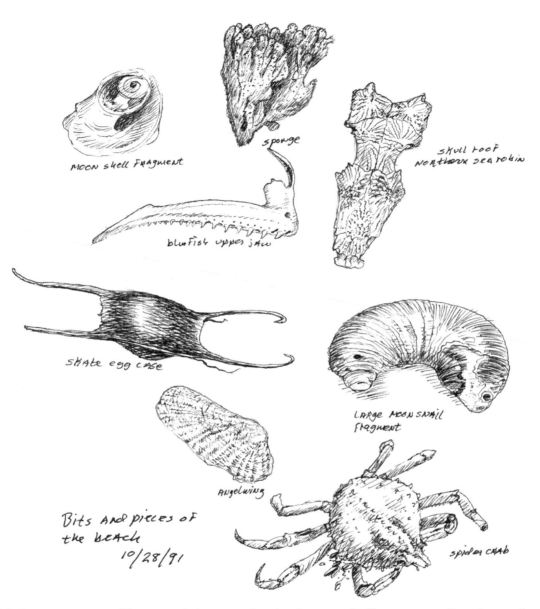

moon shell fragment

sponge

skull roof
Northern sea robin

bluefish upper jaw

skate egg case

large moon snail
fragment

Angelwing

Bits and pieces of
the beach
10/28/91

spider crab

Tide-line treasure trove. *These natural objects were found in the course of a fifteen-minute walk on the oceanfront beach. All show, to some degree or another, the endless cycle of the sea and its reclaiming powers. I was most interested in the bizarre-looking, intricately filigreed skullcap of the sea robin. Although I knew it was part of the skeletal anatomy of a fish of some kind, I had never seen such an odd design—almost as though an artist had patiently worked the little piece of bone with a stylus to attain the incredibly complex pattern of radiated lines and sculpted starbursts. An ichthyologist friend later identified it for what it was, and the next day, when walking along the beach in the same area, I found four more of the odd little plates.*

An avalanche of debris. *"The widespread beach erosion and damage to seawalls and roads could qualify the storm as one of the most serious natural disasters ever to strike the Shore area."* So proclaimed the Asbury Park Press *in the wake of the nor'easter of 1991, one of the most powerful nonhurricanes to hit the New Jersey coast in fifty years. Tides in the Shark River estuary averaged eight feet above normal over a two-day period, flooding many low-lying areas and forcing some 350 residents to flee their homes. The "big blow" was actually an oceanic tropical storm that lingered offshore for two days, bringing northeast winds and high tides to nearly the entire East Coast. One of the aftereffects was the avalanche of debris that came ashore, mostly timbers, lumber, and other flotables of incredible variety. I sketched this scene of wild disorder on the ocean beach, a strong breeze thrumming in my ears under a sky running with ragged, ominous clouds, though the storm had passed to the southeast. The removal of this tangled mass of timber—which weighed many tons—would require heavy equipment and cost thousands of dollars. The state no longer allows such unsightly flotsam to be simply burned on the beach. This section of shorefront is privately owned, and the victim—who bemusedly watched me render this sketch—told me he was resigned to allowing the mess to stay put in the hope that the next blow would deliver it farther down the coast and thus make it somebody else's problem.*

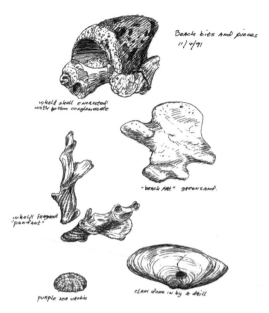

Beach bits and pieces
11/4/91

whelk shell encrusted
with bottom conglomerate

"beach art" greensand.

whelk fragment
"pendant"

purple sea urchin

clam done in by a drill

Beach "art." *An ancient whelk shell encrusted with a lump of solidified, conglomerate bottom muck (upper drawing) illustrates a mollusk's departure on the journey to fossilhood. The blackish fragments in the mud lump are bits and pieces of terrestrial wood that sank to the sea bottom and became embedded in the mass. A wave-worn piece of greensand, or green marl (lower drawing) takes on the appearance of an abstract sculpture. Years of relentless scouring by waves and sand have given the marl a delightfully smooth, natural patina that's surprisingly pleasant to the touch.*

the deserved reputation as one of the fightin'est fish in the sea. It is perhaps Shark River's preeminent game fish; only the winter flounder rivals it in popularity with anglers. Indeed, pound for pound, nothing that swims, not even the great white shark, can match a twenty-pound "chopper blue" for sheer ferocity and predatory skill and determination. Among the world's

imperiled fish—and there are many—the blue has managed to hold its own in the face of the combined threats of marine pollution and an intense and unrelenting recreational and commercial fishery throughout its vast range.

The highest praise for the mighty blues comes from the very anglers who seek to do them in. "Bluefish are not like other fish. You get the feeling they don't give a damn about you and they will bite your hand to prove it, if given

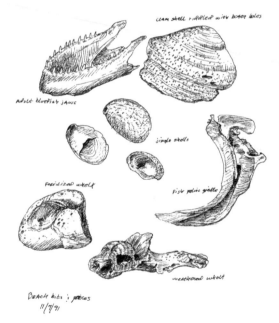

clam shell riddled with borer holes

adult bluefish jaws

jingle shells

fossilized whelk

fish pelvic girdle

weathered whelk

Beach bits & pieces
11/7/91

Treasures found on a beach walk in late fall. *From top to bottom: the sturdy, well-armed, all-business lower jaws of an adult bluefish; an old clamshell riddled with boring worm holes; three species of jingle shells; yellowfin tuna pelvic girdle; and an extremely weathered whelk shell on its way to becoming part of the beach sand.*

herring gull; head detail
11/6/91

Bird portraits. *The head study of an adult herring gull (upper drawing) was made of a bird perched nonchalantly on a dock piling not eight feet distant. The piling was close by, but off the end of the dock, so the gull seemed aware that the mini-gulf of water prevented any closer approach on the part of friend or foe, and so it calmly stayed put. This is not the case when one approaches gulls gathered on the beach.*

I've noticed that at a distance of roughly fifty feet, the birds evince general nervousness, and the flock will usually take flight if human or beast comes much closer than that. One can always pick out a disabled or sick bird on the strand at a considerable distance by its habit of running the moment it spots a beach stroller. Such unfortunates, of course, recognize their extreme vulnerability and seek to put as much distance as possible between themselves and the potential threat, and at the earliest opportunity.

A rather forlorn-looking pair of Forster's terns (lower drawing) was huddled on the upper beach—somewhat late in the year for these fair-weather creatures. These birds were virtually invisible on the shell-littered sand, and I would have passed them by had not one of them raised its wings in a luxurious stretch. I was able to gradually go into a squat and work up a fairly detailed sketch while the terns dozed on not fifteen feet away.

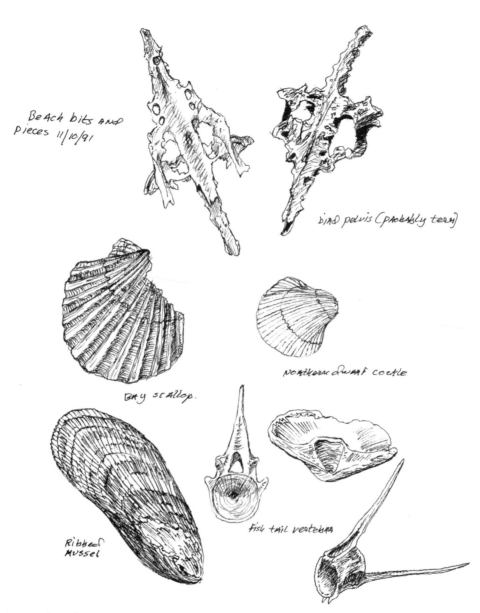

Beach bits and Pieces 11/10/91

bird pelvis (probably tern)

northern dwarf cockle

Bay scallop.

Ribbed Mussel

Fish tail vertebra

Bits and pieces found on a beach walk. Top: *At first, this curious artifact baffled me. Looking like the skull of some bizarre, exotic, little-known fish species, it had a lacy delicacy about it that gave a hint to the amount of time it had spent rolling about in the giant gem polisher of the surf. An ornithologically oriented friend later identified it as the spine and pelvis of a bird, probably a tern but just as possibly a common street pigeon. Center: The ordinary bay scallop and the northern dwarf cockle are two shells that don't seem to turn up on New Jersey beaches all that much anymore. Bottom: The section of tail vertebra is probably from an albacore. To its left is the surf-abraded shell butt, or umbo, of a large surf clam. This shell remnant did not seem to have been broken but rather worn away by the patient, everlasting action of wave and sand.*

Wind patterns. *Parking lots don't often offer the artist much in the way of promising subject material, but this one, within a stone's throw of the oceanfront, happened to be bordered by vegetation that had been rather artfully trimmed by nature. In particular, this tree clearly shows the effects of the prevailing onshore winds and salt spray. Its seaward branches, to the left, have been sculpted in a pronounced slant up and away from the beach; the branches on this side of the tree grow much more densely than those on the landward side. This is due to the toxic nature of salt, which kills the outermost buds, pruning back the branches and causing them to extend numerous branchlets in an attempt to deflect the spray and protect the tree as a whole.*

Migrating sandpipers. *A crowd of migrating semipalmateds convey a sense of manic urgency in virtually every activity they undertake. Zipping by over beach or mudflat, twisting and turning, the delightful creatures flicker and flash like tiny aerial semaphores as white undersides and then dark backs come into view. A group frenetically probing the exposed mudflats is very much akin to a mob of lilliputian sewing machines, all going at full speed, as the tiny bills excise from the beach the minute fare the birds seek. At some subtle yet mutually shared signal, the entire flock flashes into flight and sprints away like leaves before a gale—on to the next feeding place at breathtaking speed.*

Peregrine! *Even a rickety barbed wire dock barricade could not diminish this regal bird's subtle majesty and aura of silent menace. Every other bird within sight seemed acutely aware of the presence of this magnificent predator; from starlings and street pigeons to the gulls, they avoided the immediate vicinity of the pier and yet seemed irresistibly drawn to it. In short, furtive forays, the pigeons and starlings played a perilous game of "falcon roulette," repeatedly approaching low along the pier, perching below the hawk, necks craning and chattering quietly, and then hightailing it low over the sand, back toward the safety of the boardwalk. The falcon ignored them, until, becoming more restive in the sun's growing light, it dropped from its perch and flew swiftly up the beach. As it went, the crowds of gulls at rest on the sands silently took flight and hurriedly fled from its path.*

the chance." So writes John Geiser, a local fishing columnist who knows both bluefish and the Shark River fishery for them as well as any person. Although a large bluefish (up to twenty-five pounds) will surely savage all but the stoutest tackle, most fall short of the writer's tongue-in-cheek claim that "big blues strike [the bait] with a crunch that can almost be heard on the boat."

Bluefish of all stages of growth move with the tides, be they the great pelagic currents of the far, offshore deeps or those coastal eddies that gently fill the harbors and bays of summer with the six-hour cycle of new life. I have spent so much time diving and snorkeling in the company of bluefish that I can draw them nearly from memory. Though lacking in striking color or pattern, the living bluefish is attractively hued in the colors of its realm. A subtle yet beautiful sea green above, fading to bright silvery-white on the sides and belly, *Pomatomus* slips like muscled, streamlined quicksilver through the sun-shot waters of the summer sea with a grace and fluidity that's hard to match in any other living fish.

One dog-day afternoon in August lives on in my memory. I had spent much of my diving time among the forest of dock pilings lining Shark River's main channel, lazily flippering in and among the dim, shadowy, kelp-adorned supports on the ebb tide. Accompanied only by the rhythmic

Winter loon just off the north jetty at the inlet. *Bracing myself against a steady, cold ten-knot breeze out of the northeast, I contemplated the heroics involved in sketching it. Commitment to the task at hand won out, and the drawing demostrates that a viable sketch can be produced with frozen digits if one works with the greatest possible dispatch and economy of lines!*

Ill-mannered gulls. *Gulls of all species are not exactly known for their genteel table manners. The big, brash, and brawling herring and black-backed gulls are among the all-time champs in the "boarding-house reach" department. Walking the ocean beach at dawn one day, I saw that a big bruiser of a black-back had somehow secured a live, ten-inch bunker (officially called menhaden) and was in the process of beating the life out of it on the sand when it was surrounded and besieged by about a dozen of its flock fellows. Braying and croaking, it attempted to defend its prize, but there were too many competitors, and after almost losing the fish to an especially agile herring gull, it hastily swallowed the still-living fish. Getting the bunker down took a singular act of will and throat muscle, and for about ten minutes thereafter, the big gull was forced to stand stiffly, its head and neck stretched skyward at an unnatural angle until the hapless fish worked its way down to its ultimate destiny.*

A few minutes later I saw another gull drop into the surf and come up with what looked like a succulent shedder crab. As it shook the water from its feathers and flew off, it was at once set upon by a couple of hopefuls who tailed it closely, trying to force it to drop the crab. The chase soon attracted other gulls, so that the successful crabber was now ducking and dodging at least six hungry pursuers, all right behind it. The wild chase moved out over the sea and then back over the beach; gradually, most of the would-be meal stealers dropped astern, but one especially persistent pest finally jostled our hero and snatched the seafood right out of its bill.

"Mud peep" at rest on the low-tide flats.

STAR CORAL ON
GREENSAND "FREE FORMS."
11/15/91

Greensand, or marl—a common sight on New Jersey's beaches, especially after a blow. *Numerous examples of this soft, sedimentary rock were scattered over the beach at Belmar in the wake of the two fierce autumn storms that had hit the coast. Many had intriguing configurations of worm holes and wave-sculpted contours; these two examples were especially interesting. The first (upper sketch) was the largest colony of star coral I'd ever found, attached to a smooth greensand lump. The second (lower sketch) was a typically small colony, but the once-tiny worm hole had been opened up by the relentless action of the waves so that the rock and coral artifact had the look of some sort of marine bottle opener.*

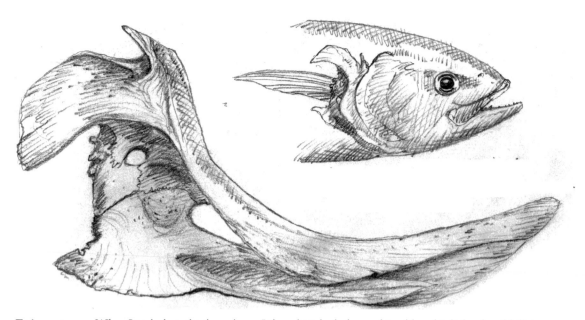

Fish anatomy. *When I picked up this large bone, I thought it looked something like a bird's head and bill; in actuality, it's the pectoral girdle of a large fish, most probably a yellowfin tuna. I've drawn the bone in its proper place in the body of the living fish—just behind the gill plate, or operculum. The girdle serves as the support for the fish's saberlike pectoral fins.*

sounds of my own breathing through the snorkel tube and the occasional disembodied, tinny whirring noises of boat motors transmitted through the water, I watched milling flocks of little cunners and blackfish swirling about over the bottom, energetically probing the dense, variegated marine growth for edibles. Numberless creatures occupied this small part of the underwater world.

The temperate littoral environment, although not as colorful or diverse as that of the tropics, harbors a richer assemblage of life in the sheer numbers of the biomass, much of it hued in the practical colors of concealment—

somber reds, browns, and greens. But in the shallow waters of the estuary or about the docks of the channel, what color there is presents itself to the eye with a rich profusion.

As I stroked easily about among the docks, the tide had been on the ebb, moving smoothly toward the sea, burbling and rolling in gentle swell, hurrying past the pilings and carrying with it all manner of land-borne debris—natural and otherwise. This particular aspect of modern diving one tends to get used to: sharing the waters with "objets de Styrofoam," cans and bottles of varied capacity, and all other species of plastic flotable delights, and gathering skills in how to elude and duck them. The moving water that day was also fairly turbid—visibility at perhaps eight feet—and most of this aquatic "smaze" was a distressing combination of natural effluents leached from the marshes inland and the land-borne runoff that daily invades the estuary from the streets and byways of the surrounding Shark River Hills region.

Al Rooney, a local diver who grew up on the river, recalls with bittersweet memory the estuary of a mere thirty years ago when "you could lay on top and see the bottom—fifteen or twenty feet deep—then in four or five years you couldn't see anything . . . the pollution changed rapidly in the 1960s." Today Rooney still plumbs the estuary's depths when he has a notion to, but he

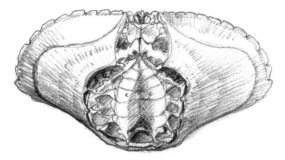

The geometric perfection of a rock crab's plastron. *Examination of this well-preserved crab shell showed the interior to be a maze of supporting struts and braces outdoing in efficient complexity the most sophisticated human engineering feat!*

notes that "when the tide's coming in you can see twenty feet underwater. For ten minutes, it's still, then it turns around outgoing, and you can't see a thing—you can see the pollution in the river like a fogbank coming at you." This is stuff that will make you sick, if you're careless, and many a diver, this one included, has had some lengthy bouts of illness following a swim in the river when the fecal coliform count has been way up there.

But luck was with me that day in August; the outgoing aquatic haze was a mere ethereal scrim compared to what it could have been, and the tide was near ebb and on the verge of turning. One could almost see the rock bottom of the cycle: the flotsam paused and circled uncertainly; the rockweed thickets splayed upward toward the light above, spreading fanlike, from their piling anchorages, and the virtual blizzard of organic debris in the water came to an easy standstill.

In the course of past dives I had often attempted to time the extent of dead low tide, but without much success. In the past it had always seemed that the great, silent pause between the inhalations and exhalations of the sea had crept by without notice—at one moment the crowds of moon jellyfish and the ethereal, oblong sea walnuts would be drifting and

Black-bellied plovers. *These big, pigeon-sized shorebirds were mercilessly hunted by market gunners in the nineteenth century, so that the vast flocks that swept up and down the coast during migration are no more. Along the Jersey shore one is more likely to see small parties of between five and a dozen birds either probing the estuary's mudflats or quietly taking their ease on the ocean beach. These individuals are in the somber grayish and white winter plumage; the spring adults are most attractive and conspicuous, being a checkered black and white above with velvety black face, neck, and underparts.*

Bonaparte's Gulls Diving For Fish
At the inlet mouth
12/16/91

detail of head

Winter gull visitors. *Walking the oceanfront just after dawn on a windy, bitter cold December day, I noticed that large numbers of the graceful, ternlike Bonaparte's gull had moved inshore and were boisterously fishing in the inlet's channel. The little "Boney" is a common winter gull here at Shark River, and unlike the larger and more gregarious herring, black-backed, and ring-billed species, it pretty much keeps to itself. This excited flock was cruising along the rocks of the north jetty, its members making repeated plunges into the surging brine after some unidentified small fish swimming near the surface. On diving, the birds would submerge completely, a rather unusual feat for a gull, for only the kittiwake has the ability to both dive and swim after the finned prey it seeks.*

Owing to the daunting wind and penetrating cold, I roughed these sketches in in pencil and then finished them later in pen. I used a "Sharpie" permanent marker for the broad, shadowed areas of the rocks and a Bic "Micro Metal" pen for the finer details of the upper rocks and the birds themselves.

Holding back the sea. *Much of the northern New Jersey shore is far from being the littoral primeval but rather has been buttressed and reinforced against the assault of the sea by manmade constructions. Most of this construction takes the form of jetties, groins, and bulkheads, but in some areas, such as this artificial bluff near Shark River Inlet, huge blocks of concrete highway demolition rubble have been dumped and backfilled at the edge of the land to form an enduring berm. Although certainly not picturesque in the traditional sense of the word, this weed-and-rubble tangle hosts a surprising amount of small wildlife. On the brisk and windy New Year's Day I sketched it, the place was alive with song sparrows and juncos, furtively foraging among the dried dune grass and seaside goldenrod.*

bobbling in one direction, toward the inlet, and in the next, back toward the harbor. Or at the slack tide the warmish, debris-laden waters of the emptying bay suddenly and almost miraculously cleared as lunar muscle stayed the flow and then levered the sea back up the narrow channel.

This time the turning was less a visual event than it was one of tactile impressions, in particular, those of heat and cold. On that particular August day the water's temperature hovered around seventy-six degrees Fahrenheit, for the most part the result of its six-hour stay in the shallow, sun-heated estuary. As the mass of seawater began to press in through the channel from the outside ocean, I felt the great, liquid volume shift landward, not with force, but with a gentle though compelling persuasion. I took a breath and went under, flippering down to the sandy substrate that lay about eight feet below. At once I got the unmistakable "feel" of the tide as I was punched by an astonishingly cold thermocline slipping invisibly along the bottom; the frigid water layer lent graphic truth to the fact that the average temperature of the oceans worldwide is a mere thirty-nine degrees Fahrenheit.

At the van of the chilled, bottle-green flow came a little flock of spots, a small marine fish a.k.a. the lafayette here in New Jersey. The little fish, one

A lone beach walker at dawn, putting a large flock of gulls to flight. *By January, none but the hardiest of strollers brave the winter beach at Belmar, though the nearby boardwalk may be thronged with walkers and runners of all ages and Spandex colors.*

The beach in winter here presents an interesting visual paradox: stand facing the sea and the scene is one of wild beauty. The broad, uncluttered ocean and the vast expanse of eastern sky, ever-changing and always glorious, the swirling, noisy presence of the birds of the sea, whether they be the omnipresent gulls or the less common avian folk like loons or sea ducks, combine to offer the viewer a time-traveler's glimpse of the planet's distant, prehuman past. Turn, now, and take in the western vista: a north-to-south conglomeration of shoreside resort hotels, once stately rooming houses, private homes, and colorful beachfront tourist traps, all lined up safely behind that single most popular of beachfront human habitats—the ever-busy boardwalk. I would suspect that it is nearly impossible to gain so striking a contrast between the natural and manmade elements of the earth anywhere else by simply turning about in place!

private dock at low tide.

Drift timbers on the beach

Docks and drift timbers. *Wood, in the aspect of both construction and destruction, is a prominent feature of the Shark River seascape. The "back side" is punctuated here and there along its marshy length by aged and rickety, though often picturesque, private docks that may or may not survive the year's hurricane season!*

Wood may also be present both on the oceanfront and in the estuary in a not-so-aesthetic form—that of drift timbers. This large-scale debris has as its source either ancient and decrepit docks up-coast that simply break up in storms and drift far and wide, or the big barges that, until recently, hauled dock and land-based demolition debris several miles offshore for burning. When present en masse, drift timbers are more an eyesore than an environmental hazard; they have been implicated in a number of injuries and deaths stemming from boat collisions at night or in foul weather. Timbers that have lain on the upper beach for several years weather to an almost attractive silvery-gray and become a sort of manmade habitat for small wildlife. I've found a wide variety of insect and small mammal species in residence in some older timbers that have almost merged into the natural landscape over time.

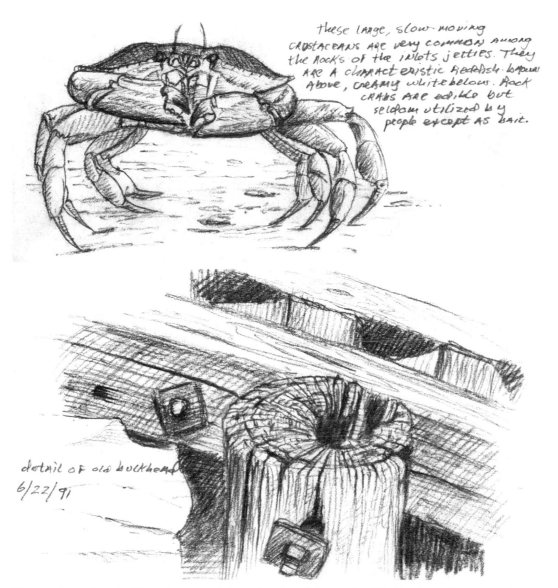

these large, slow-moving crustaceans are very common among the rocks of the inlets jetties. They are a characteristic reddish-brown above, creamy white below. Rock crabs are edible but seldom utilized by people except as bait.

detail of old bulkhead
6/22/91

Rescue of a rock crab. *These drawings of the rock crab and the weathered bulkhead would appear to have no real connection, but they do in the sense that this animal was found, in a state of torpid dehydration, among the rocks at the wall's base. It had, no doubt, been tossed there by a disgusted angler who had foul-hooked it on the line. Before liberating the crab back to the sea, I enjoyed drawing its portrait while I held the creature in my left hand; it was, out of character for the species, a most cooperative subject.*

The bulkhead piling interested me because its top showed clearly the weathering effect of wind and wave. The moist salt air and the high-tide pounding of the surf had destroyed the soft wood between the harder grains of the piling clear down through its core. The big bolts securing the piling to the seawall were likewise corroded to a bright red, flaking rust—all in the space of less than three decades.

Purple sand pipers
4aark River Inlet jetty

Purple sandpipers. *These shorebirds appeared to be more abundant than usual in 1992, perhaps due to the warm winter? These chunky little "rock peeps" are usually seen here in parties of between four and ten individuals; I came across this large flock—with many birds coming and going all the time—alternately resting and energetically probing the surprisingly lush crop of green alga coating the low-tide oceanfront jetty rocks at the inlet's mouth. The purple sandpiper is a tame, confiding bird and allows a fairly close approach—a bonanza for the artist hoping for a "fast draw" on a cold, windy winter day! I drew these guys in pencil.*

of the drum and croaker tribe, seemed to be at the vanguard of the invading sea, materializing out of the pale green distance and probing and scooting across the channel's floor in nervous, darting sorties, their deep-bodied, silvery forms nearly as transient and elusive as the ever-shifting sun-dappled sand bottom itself. Spot are timorous creatures, flitting away and out of sight at the first approach of a diver.

Drifting up the channel, I scanned the seascape passing slowly beneath me and noticed that, oddly, the bustle of fish activity I'd noted on the ebb tide had suddenly ceased; the spots had abruptly come together into a tight little bunch and then skittered off across the sand into the submarine distance, and most of the smaller fishes that had filled the water with their food-gathering industry moments before had vanished. Not a fin remained in sight among the tangles of wrack and rockweed, these now leaning with the current in an up-channel direction.

It was as though all life and motion had been locked into a rigid suspension, in breathless anticipation of some unknown, vaguely sinister impending event.

Puzzled, I paused and swung about in midwater—and at once saw the reason for this abrupt suspension of activity: I was at the head of one of the largest schools of harbor blues I had seen in the channel in a long time. A veritable wall of fish confronted me, moving up-channel, occupying the view from the water's surface to the sandy bottom eight feet below. Threading their way in and out of the pilings, passing below the dark, whalelike, gently swaying hulls of anchored boats,

Bluefish invasion! *Obviously, this is a drawing from memory! I think the drawing, executed with an ordinary No. 2 Eberhard & Faber pencil, conveys the exceptional clarity of the water that hot August day as well as the silent, almost dignified procession of the fish as they approached and then passed by me. They seemed not at all fazed by the sudden appearance of a rather large, cumbersome creature in their midst; as the wall of fish swept past, I felt myself under the impassive scrutiny of a hundredfold cold, round eyes that seemed to appraise me, pass some unknown, fishy judgment, and then slip by and vanish in the soft, green haze ahead.*

Feeding frenzy. *The scene shown in this drawing is one of those "mini-events" of nature that occurs with frequency on the estuary during those lazy, hazy days of mid- and late summer. In July and August, Shark River is filled from shore to shore with vast schools of silversides, anchovies, and other smaller fish. These are prey for a host of other creatures, including the terns and the bluefish. Young blues, locally called "snappers," follow the great shoals of silversides about the estuary and attack them almost continuously from below. The resulting aquatic mayhem, highly visible when the bay is flat and calm, attracts the terns from far and wide, and they join in the fray, diving and swirling overhead in great excitement.*

the fish swam at a leisurely pace yet were clearly intent on reaching a destination; the bluefish were moving into the estuary to feed on the great swarms of spearing and anchovies that found tenuous refuge there.

Anyone who has spent any time behind a pair of binoculars in the pursuit of the fine art of birding knows that smaller birds will effect a hasty but furtive exit on the approach of a predator such as a hawk or owl. Retreat is the better part of valor under such circumstances, and among the lesser fishes of the edge of the sea, there are few that will engage in a contest of wills

with a bluefish. And there were many, many of them moving up the channel with me on that cold, incoming sea.

The so-called harbor blue is that sized fish between the juvenile snapper blue (up to about thirteen inches) and the oceangoing adult bluefish, a.k.a. chopper, alligator, or horse. The average harbor bluefish will range between fourteen and twenty inches, and most run around three to five pounds. Even at these modest dimensions, a bluefish is not a creature to be trifled with, as any smaller marine creature that has managed to survive to maturity is well aware.

snapper blues in action

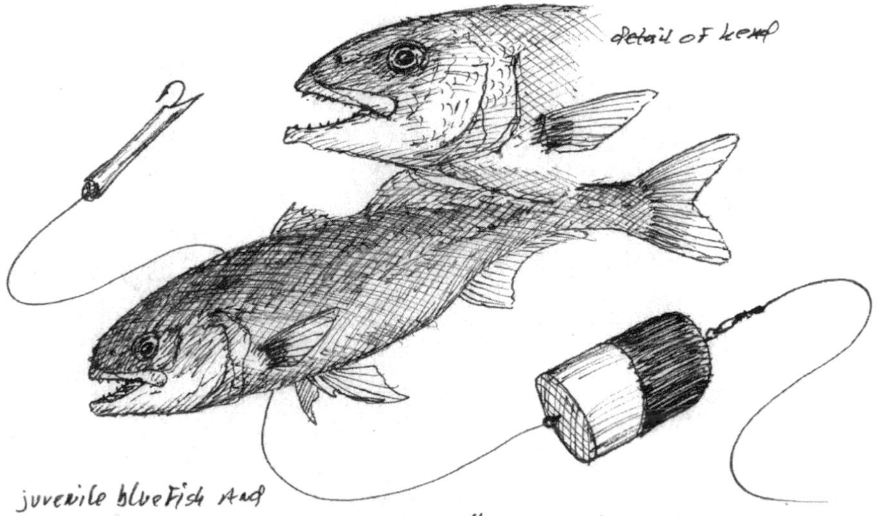

detail of head

juvenile bluefish and

The "snapper bluefish." *Here is one of the staples of the Shark River recreational fishery. The snapper blue is defined as a juvenile bluefish up to about nine or ten inches in length; bluefish up to three or four pounds are called harbor blues, or tailor blues, while the seagoing adults are known as school blues, "alligators," or "choppers"— depending on the locality. The bluefish is capable of almost phenomenal growth under favorable conditions (meaning an abundance of prey); a four-inch snapper may more than double that size in a single growing season, and by the end of its second year it may be twenty-four inches long and weigh six pounds. This factor, added to the blue's fighting spirit and formidable appetite, combine to make it a premier gamefish up and down the East Coast.*

The feeding-action sketch (top) is a quick impression of movements that occurred almost too quickly for the eye to follow. The drawing of the bluefish (bottom) was made from a "fish in hand" destined for the frying pan.

My companions in the channel that day appeared to be at the upper end of the harbor blue size range, and as the school overtook me, dividing and passing on either side, I was struck by their classic bluefish "attitude." One thing that really can't be said of a fish's eye is that it conveys a wide range of emotions. But being eyeballed by many hundreds of round-eyed, "expressionless" bluefish did something to my terrestrial psyche down there that day! Those cold, piscine eyes, row upon row, rank upon rank of them. What thoughts, if in fact they could be so-called, coursed through those tiny, predatory brains?

These creatures, accustomed to the open sea, a world lacking boundaries or physical constraints, were now navigating a narrow channel fringed with docks, walled in by bulkheads, and afloat with pleasure boats and debris. A foraging—indeed, hunting—submarine army on the move, passing in utter silence but communicating its advance far and wide through the conductivity of the water world itself.

In spite of the blue's utilitarian, streamlined, fusiform body, designed strictly for speed and exquisite maneuverability in the fish's watery realm, there is a definite milieu, a "personality" conveyed by the fish, especially when they appear in great numbers. "Menace" is not quite the

right word for it, for even the largest bluefish has neither the size nor the threatening mien of a shark, but rather a barely controlled ferocity. Even the most dangerous shark is a rather goofy, dopey creature when sated, given to lazily planing and blundering about and generally minding its own business. A shark comes to life when appetite plus the proper stimuli trigger its alter ego, at which time it instantly becomes an eager, questing, and determined predator. Bluefish, on the other hand, seem to have something on their minds all the time. This may be due to their tight schooling behavior, in which each and every member of the school is finely attuned to the doings of the others, but a disciplined squadron of bluefish is not a gaggle of timorous shiners, make no mistake about it. The great crowd of them that passed by me flank to flank on that August day were well aware of my presence, as well as that of every other living thing within sight and sound wave. They were splendid, those iron-jawed, sea-green-and-silver phantoms, magically suspended in the clear, flowing, liquid universe, coming in from the wide and windy sea lanes into the small estuary. Indeed the stuff of art and poetry, the bluefish, and I have sketched and painted the enigmatic creature many times over in my years near the sea, never having lost my appreciation for

Blues "Finning".
This pod of 3-5 lb
blues was simply
cruising, looking for
bunkers, or menhaden,
to pursue.

"Tailor," or Harbor bluefish
approx 6 lbs.
caught May 19th 92
on the oceanfront at
Deal.

Bluefish
(Pomatomus saltatrix)

Fishing season begins! *My 1992 fishing season came in, literally, with a bang, with the capture of four nice "tailor" bluefish in the surf not far from the Shark River Inlet. The fish averaged five pounds, just the right size for the table, in my opinion, for the larger chopper blues are too oily and reputed to be carrying residues of heavy metals and other such toxic delights. I released two of the fish, keeping the others for the family larder, and decided to draw the head of one of them, so noble and wild did it appear even in death.*

The bluefish is yet another marine species that has come under catch regulation; there is no size limit for the species, but anglers may possess no more than ten fish per day within New Jersey territorial waters. Most recreational anglers have no objection to this limit, but the ruling has come under fire as a hardship to low-income folk, who will often pool their resources and send one of their number on a fishing trip to stock up on fresh fish for the neighborhood.

its supremely imposing presence and life-style.

I once watched a large school of bluefish in the gentle swells just off the beach on a "bluebird day" in late summer some years ago. The water was marvelously clear, and the fish, at least a hundred of them, were moving slowly up and down the beach near a popular fishing jetty, languidly riding the rising curl of the mild surf, just loafing along. They seemed to be simply celebrating their complete mastery of their element, moving in to within yards of the beach, letting the swells lift them and "body surf" them in and out with the pull of the water. Their presence so close to the rocks had not gone unreported among the local fishermen, for before long a crowd of hopeful anglers lined the jetty, frantically flinging lures and baits of a dozen varieties into the middle of the throng of fish. It would have seemed an easy slaughter, but the fish completely ignored all the efforts to deceive and capture them; no matter the bait presented or the artful manner of retrieve—right through the center of the school—not a fish rose to the bait. And ten minutes later they were gone, as one, abruptly turning and moving seaward along the flank of the jetty and disappearing into the open sea beyond.

Part II

10/3/91

High Noon; Low Tide; Clams

Low tide afternoc
APRIL

A low-tide afternoon on the estuary. *This scene is pretty much dominated by birds. Extreme low water, whether it occurs early in the season, as in this scene, or during the busy Fourth of July weekend in a rip-roaring summer on the Jersey shore, is notable for the lack of boat traffic on the estuary. Water depth throughout the bay averages about four feet at high water, but as can be seen here, the topography of the estuary is rife with mud and sandbars. Most operators of larger powerboats avoid the place during extreme low water, but occasionally, the adventurous skipper of a deep-keeled sailboat will attempt passage to dock and often gets hung up on a bar. Depending on the force of the grounding, a stranded craft may be towed or shoved off the bar, or, more likely, its occupants may have to resign themselves to a two- or three-hour wait for the next tide.*

The eternal rise and fall of the sea's level on a six-hour basis is as elemental and cosmic a force as is the sun's appearance on the eastern horizon each new day. Our North Jersey shore's defiant seawalls and the resolute dikes of the Netherlands may limit the scope and span of the tide's influence for the time being, geologically speaking, but no force short of the destruction of the solar system itself can put an end to the sea's appointed invasion of the edge of the land.

Yet when the tide retreats, it lays bare the wonderful hidden life of the mudflats.

Contrary to popular belief, the temperate littoral boasts a much richer, if somewhat less diverse, array of life than tropical marine habitats. The popular image of the idyllic coral reef populated by armies of multihued fishes and bizarre invertebrates is, of course, a valid one, but the supply of nutrients is lower in the tropics owing to the relatively static water temperatures. It takes the dramatic seasonal changes and the accompanying upwelling and exchange of the water column of the middle and boreal latitudes to trigger the release of nutrients and make them available to the creatures of the temperate estuaries.

Coastal marine habitats, of both tropical and temperate ecologies, possess incredible powers of renewal in the face of degradation from both natural and human sources. This capacity for self-healing serves them well when the natural assault (such as a hurricane) is brief, or the human pressure light to moderate. Problems arise when, as in the case of Shark River, recreational and utilitarian use of an estuary become intense and prolonged. This little bay, less than two square miles in total area, is immensely popular as a place of recreation for at least half of the year and receives the nonpoint effluent (land runoff) of the surrounding region for all of the remainder.

At least one of the reasons for the rather cavalier and heavy-handed approach to modern mechanized recreation on the Shark River estuary, and indeed, on virtually every navigable bay on both coasts, is that much, if not most, of its rich and varied life remains hidden from human eyes. To most people, both residents and summer visitors alike, the little bay is simply a

Winter at the marina. *The concrete fish-cleaning table at the Belmar Marina hosts a different class of "fishermen" in the dead of winter! This dock fronts on the broad south arm of the estuary and is subject to bone-chilling winds even in midsummer, but in winter only the most dedicated (perhaps unhinged would be a better word) of anglers brave the ever-windy spot for a brace of fat winter flounder!*

I found myself lacking in artistic spine this particular day and sat in the comfort of my van, which positively shook and rocked in the thirty-knot breeze, and drew these herring gulls holding position against the gale.

broad expanse of water, flat and generally featureless salt marshes, and all that damp and fragrant mud separating the convoluted boat channels at low tide. These are some of the physical features that combine to make the estuary so visually appealing, but few people understand the complex ecology of the bay; to the majority of visitors, the bay is an aquatic playground, pure and simple.

To probe the effect of the greatly intensified human usage of the estuary over only the past two decades, one must first gain at least a lay knowledge of its ecological workings. Shark River,

2/12/92

Double-crested cormorants. *These birds eye the artist with suspicion from a shoreside bulkhead—but stay put for their portrait. This drawing, made from the rather close vantage of a riverside parking spot, illustrates perfectly the use of a motor vehicle as a "blind." Cormorants, having been persecuted by anglers in many areas, are very wary and would never allow such a close approach by a person on foot, but these birds saw at least no direct threat in my van parked nearby.*

"King Fisher Cove" 3/29/92

Reflections. *It's obvious that reflections are a prominent feature in a habitat composed primarily of water. The natural coastal environment is rather on the flat side, with little other than a low tree line to register in reflection on the water's surface; thus at Shark River the artist will find most of the "ripple pictures" to be those of docks, bridges, and moored boats. These are certainly fair game as subject material; many marine constructions have a certain appeal about them, and most of them sport avian "decor" of one species or another. In this case, as I drew the scene shown here, a kingfisher returned repeatedly to a nearby piling after each fishing foray.*

in its present configuration, is a relatively shallow body of water that may undergo extreme fluctuations in water temperature and salinity over the twelve-hour tidal cycle. Although lacking the relatively stable environmental conditions of the much larger Barnegat Bay to the south, this former river mouth is nonetheless a rich aquatic seedbed for the plants that form the foundation for the vast and intricate network of life that rises from it, terminating in the largest and most visible organisms—the myriad seabirds, and the oceanic fishes that ultimately serve as food for humankind.

The estuary's fishes are tied to myriad forms of life in their environment by food chains, or webs. Whether they be herbivores or carnivores, the root of their very existence will be found in the plants— either the larger, more visible types, such as eelgrass or spartina, or those minute, single-celled atoms of life that exist in the bay in the countless billions— the algae. This is the very soup of life, without which nothing else on earth can survive. The bugs and the fishes, the birds and the beasts, and people as well, utterly depend on the humblest of creation for their collective and personal futures. Damage or destroy this universe of planktonic wanderers, this immense base of the food pyramid, and all else right to its apex will follow it into oblivion as surely as the sun rises above the inlet each day.

Healthy plant growth is directly and adversely affected by both physical destruction and by declining water quality. One of the more pressing problems currently facing the intricate plant communities of the estuary is the direct damage inflicted by powerboat props and jetskis. A fair percentage of the Shark River estuary is covered by less than four feet of water at mean high tide. The substrate in most of these areas is soft sand or mud,

Nailing tuna tails to slip pilings—a common practice among charter boat owners everywhere. *The object being both a good-luck offering and an advertisement of the particular skipper's proficiency in locating the famous gamefish at sea. I thought this collection of caudal appendages had an oddly primitive, almost totemic look to it. These tails, probably those of yellowfin and bigeye tunas, had obviously been in place for several years; they were bleached by the sun and virtually mummified by the drying effects of the seaside elements.*

Death on the shore. *This drawing, which tells an all-too-familiar tale today, is one of the more unpleasant and painful ones I've executed, and for a very personal reason. The day before, I came across this unfortunate herring gull standing in the roadway with its head and bill encased in the grip of one of those obscene sixpack rings. The bird was weak but still had enough strength to elude my attempt to capture it and remove the plastic; it laboriously flew off over the bay while I, in frustration and sadness, stood and watched it go. Although I tried to track the bird's flight, I lost sight of it . . . until the next morning, when I found it freshly dead on a bulkhead across the cove. Filled with anger against this "legacy" of humankind at the edge of the sea, I made this drawing and then, I felt prompted to at least cut away the offending junk and give the unfortunate creature a decent burial in the flank of a nearby dune. Somehow, I felt better for offering that rather useless but necessary atonement for the sin of one of my own against a nameless bird.*

main channel marker

The Shark River Inlet and estuary, one of the busiest on the New Jersey shore. *Here is anchorage for a sizable commercial fishing and lobstering fleet and numerous pleasure craft. Its main channel, although of a zigzag configuration, is well marked with buoys and standing channel markers; experienced boaters wisely avoid other areas of the broad, shallow bay, but occasionally a "weekend mariner" will become adventurous at the wrong tide and get hung up on the wide mudflats.*

The rotted remains of the old Shark River Park boardwalk (lower sketch) stretch for about a half-mile along the estuary's western shore, fronting South Riverside Drive. At the turn of the century several small hotels and a marina were located there, and the twenty-foot-wide boardwalk rivaled those of the North Jersey oceanfront in popularity; all that remain now are jagged, barnacle- and kelp-encrusted supports and planking.

or a combination of the two—sometimes referred to, logically enough, as "smud."

Much of the "smud," or at least those areas of it nearer the shoreline, are often lushly vegetated in dense beds of spartina, eelgrass, widgeon grass, three-corner rush, black grass, and other submerged and emergent estuarine plants that in turn support a vast array of micro- and macroscopic animals, from diatoms to grass shrimp. None of the shallower grassy areas of the estuary are protected or posted in any way except when they happen to be located near docks and marinas, whereby they are given incidental protection under the sporadically obeyed "No Wake" (six knots) rule.

Given the density of the bay's

BAnded Rudderfish (young)
7/4/91

A young banded rudderfish. *In drawing a shallow water eelgrass and spartina bed, I came across something of an unusual sight among the plant tangle. This species of fish is of a distinctly pelagic nature, that is, normally found in open water, usually in the ocean, so it was a surprise to see the strikingly patterned fish so close to shore and in such shallow water. At first I thought it was in distress for it allowed a very close approach (I was able to touch it briefly), but then I saw the fish make swift, darting sorties into the weed beds and noticed that it was hunting small fishes and the abundant grass shrimp. After each foray, it would return to one particular spot among the submerged plants and hover there, waiting for passing prey.*

This species is closely related to the pilot fish and like that species often accompany sharks, sea turtles, and other large animals, including human divers. I have had rudderfish escort me many times while diving; they usually position themselves right under one's chest or close behind a shoulder, sometimes swimming directly in front of the diving mask's faceplate! They are very curious and even friendly creatures, quite unafraid of a human being in their own environment.

Rain on the river. Black ducks
huddle under gray skies and a
steady rain
7/27/91

Disabled Lion's mane jellyfish

In the rain. *Rain has many and varied effects on the creatures of the estuary. For one thing, an intense storm will affect the salinity of the water and alter the behavior patterns of many aquatic creatures; some fishes retreat toward the inlet and the ocean during periods of very heavy rainfall, while others, such as the brackish-water mummichog, or common killifish, are attracted to the fresh water and appear closer to the shoreline and near drain outfalls. Most of the estuary's waterfowl simply stay where they are and ride out the foul weather.*

For some reason, in the day or two following a coastal storm, stranded jellyfish seem to be more in evidence than under normal conditions. This may perhaps result from the physical buffeting the wind and waves subject the fragile, watery animals to, as well as the sudden change in the salinity of inshore waters. I found this large lion's mane jelly bobbing helplessly about in shallow water on an incoming tide. It was attended by a small fish— probably a young jack—that clung very closely to the big coelenterate, even swimming up inside its large, rounded "bell." The fish can be seen in the drawing as a darkish shadow in the lower edge of the jellyfish's bell. When I visited the beach later in the day, the lion's mane had stranded above the high-tide line and was nothing more than a flattened mass of translucent goo.

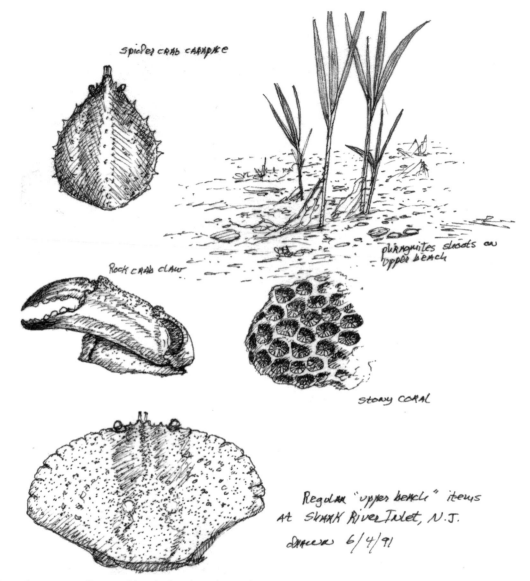

spider crab carapace

phragmites shoots on upper beach

rock crab claw

stony coral

Regular "upper beach" items at Shark River Inlet, N.J.
Sauer 6/4/91

Natural treasures. *Regrettably, the beachcomber walking the shoreline anywhere in or near the New York metropolitan area is often likely to come across artifacts other than the natural, for the problem of manmade flotsam and jetsam has become one of great concern in recent years. Owing to relatively effective legislation and the efforts of conservation groups in the shore area, the litter plague has abated over the past three years, so that natural objects like those shown in this sketch may be collected with less fear of coming into contact with noxious or even dangerous trash on the beaches.*

One of the more common, yet unusual, beach finds is the bleached remains of the stony coral, or star coral. A true coral, this colonial creature is one of the northernmost corals, thriving in rocky offshore habitats in temperate waters. The whitish, intricate skeletons of the stony coral are common sea-wrack items along the New Jersey shore.

Angling for eels on the "back side." *Although the American eel, or common eel, does not enjoy much popularity as prime table fare among rank-and-file anglers, the fish does have a small but devoted following. Eel fishing is usually an all-day affair, with the anglers bringing food coolers, deck chairs, and beach umbrellas along in addition to their fishing gear for maximum comfort during the sometimes lengthy wait for a strike. Eeling is usually most productive shortly after the turn of the ebb tide, when the fish follow the bait fish up the channels.*

summer recreational boating fleet, the "avoidance (of other craft) factor" has become an even more daunting proposition for the average recreational boater, so that virtually every square yard of water surface is put to the propeller at one point or another in the tidal cycle. And this includes those shallow areas that would be considered extremely sensitive and unable to withstand a determined assault by motor craft of any type.

To understand the ultimate consequences of this destructive, albeit unintentional, environmental vandalism, one must follow the convoluted nutritional path that meanders from algae and eelgrass to shrimp, blue crab, and finally to, say, that marine superpredator, the bluefish.

A discussion of the aquatic food chain would not be complete without mention of an interesting little piece of environmental arithmetic known among

clapper rail at water's edge.
7/30/91

The clapper rail. *This is not a common marsh bird on the estuary for the overall salt-marsh area here is not extensive. I found this individual stalking slowly about in a rather exposed situation at the marsh fringe, and since it seemed in no hurry to leave I was able to get a good rendering. The bird padded sedately about, nodding its head, flicking its tail, and eyeing the shoreline for edibles. Its behavior was decidedly chickenlike, inspiring the nickname "marsh hen" for rails in general.*

    On this, the last day of July, it seemed that there were more than the usual number of small sandpipers, or "mud peep," coursing back and forth over the low-tide mudflats. Perhaps the effect of the early onset of this year's "greenhouse effect" summer and breeding season? Most of the early southward-moving migrants appeared to be sanderlings and least and semipalmated sandpipers. They fled by so low and so swiftly that I found myself able to capture only the barest essence of their tightly coordinated flight on the spot, filling in what few details I could recall long after they had passed out of sight.

common egret poses
8/1/91

Ciconiiformes. *The larger heron and egret species (the Order Ciconiiformes) are the easiest birds to sketch. Under normal circumstances they are slower, more deliberate fliers and when fishing, will often "hold a pose" for considerable periods. The great blue heron (upper sketch) was caught as it leisurely flapped its way across the estuary shortly after sunup, presenting a silhouette picture and an upside-down reflection in the water. These big, conspicuous wading birds are a common sight on the estuary, though nobody seems to know where they nest.*

Minutes later, the American, or common, egret (lower sketch) sailed in for a landing and at once began plucking small fish from the milling swarms in the shallow water. The beautiful bird was the very embodiment of intense concentration, moving slowly and methodically about and leaning forward and studying the water intently before making its quick, snakelike strike. Egrets are abundant in Shark River, though they do not breed in the immediate environs; they have adapted well to the presence of people and their aquatic toys, and appear completely unperturbed by all the human activity going on around them.

I drew this bird using an old, nearly dry Pilot razor-point pen that gave me the slightly "dry point" look I was seeking in the drawings.

Gull sick with botulism on the back side beach. when I returned four hours lat the bird had died.

7/27/91

Death of a gull. *The gulls are among the most efficient and "ruthless" predators of the coastal environment and thus terminate the lives of countless organisms during their life spans. But they, too, are mortal and reach their own end in one way or another.*

I first saw this gull in an obviously distressed state, lopsidedly trying to stay afloat, lodged underneath a dock about fifty feet from the shoreline. Later that day, I found it high on the beach and saw on close examination that it was extremely emaciated and had virtually no body fat. It was little more than a pathetic bundle of bone and feathers. Its eyes were oddly large and "glassy," and its expression had that shrunken look of acute malnutrition. I suspected botulism, the result of eating toxic organic matter gleaned from the very warm and rather stagnant waters of the upper estuary. Or perhaps it had been feeding on the largesse of a landfill somewhere. I stopped by the place four hours later and found the bird, stiff and twisted in death on the sand. Its eye was covered with debris, and the flies were already at work.

ecologists as "The Rule of Ten." It has been found that in most living organisms it requires ten unit weights of food to manufacture a single unit weight of themselves; the rule seems to work out that way in every food chain, from the highest predator all the way down to its near-microscopic source. In other words, a growing human being will gain a tenth of a pound of tissue (1.6 ounces) in the eating of one pound of bluefish. The blue in turn acquired its pound by devouring ten pounds of mackerel, which got their ten pounds by eating 100 pounds of silversides, which ate 1,000 pounds of plankton,

Storm drain outlet. *Though serving a strictly utilitarian and distinctly odious purpose, a storm drain outlet has a certain artistic appeal to it, depending on your level of appreciation for things manmade. Storm drains are the principal source of "nonpoint" pollution in the estuary; that is, contaminants not originating from a specific source, such as a factory waste outflow or oil spill. According to the Monmouth County water pollution control authorities, there are 120 such drains scattered around the shores of Shark River, and these introduce street runoff, oils, lawn chemicals, and animal feces into the estuary following exceptionally heavy rainfalls. In this regrettable state of affairs, Shark River estuary is no better or worse than other coastal tidal habitats along the East Coast.*

Angling for fluke. *Long a popular pastime at Shark River, this activity reaches its peak in August, when the tasty flatfish move into the shallow waters of coastal bays to spawn. In recent years the fluke fishery declined to the point of nonexistence as the fish all but disappeared from inshore waters. Intensive and increasing recreational and commercial fishing pressure was doubtless part of the cause of the decline, but over the past two years, the species has effected an encouraging comeback, so that hopeful "flukers" in small boats are once again a part of the estuary's summer angling scene.*

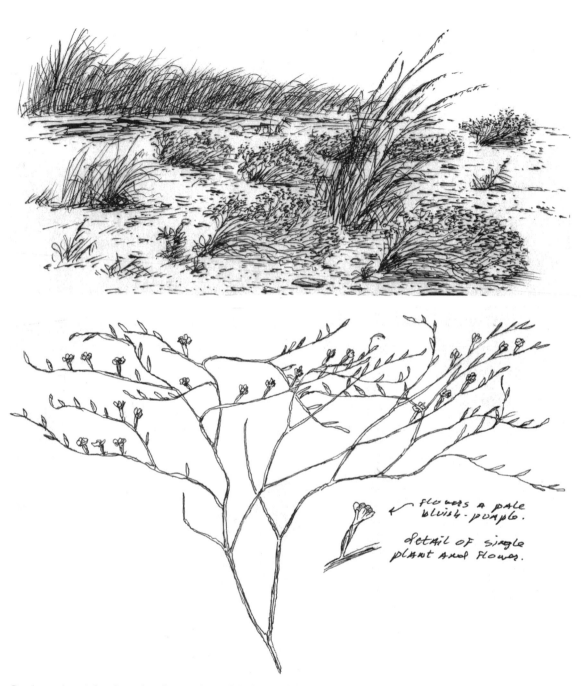

flowers a pale bluish-purple.

detail of single plant and flower.

Sea lavender. *A hardy, salt-tolerant plant of the brackish littoral, this attractive plant, with its lacy sprinkles of tiny, bright pink flowers, is a favorite of floral designers, who utilize the dried fronds in arrangements. Sea lavender is not an overly abundant plant at Shark River since its rather specialized habitat—hardpan clay just above the high-tide mark—is in relatively short supply.*

The Avian method of clam shucking — direct and right to the point. My own observations indicate that only the herring gull engages in this interesting behavior; I've never seen the other species do it.

2/13/92

The hard-shell clam, or quahog. *Fair game for the larger herring and black-backed gulls; in the smaller sizes these clams are portable and easily dropped from a height. This species is once again common in the estuary owing to the closure of the clamming industry here.*

soft-shell, or "piss clams" squint
from the low tide mudflat.
8/26/91

One of the more common Shark River bivalves—the soft-shell clam. *It is also known as the steamer, gaper, nannynose, and by the indelicate, but rather appropriate, local moniker, "piss clam." Once the object of an intense fishery, the soft-shell harvest is at this time prohibited throughout the Shark River estuary owing to overall degradation of the habitat. The state closed the river to shellfishing for the first time in 1961, and although in recent years it has been periodically reopened to clammers, all bivalves taken from the estuary during open seasons must be sent to purification beds in Great South Bay, on the south Jersey coast, before they can legally be sold.*

During the Great Depression, Shark River clams saw many a local family through some very hard times. One veteran riverman recalls: "We had clams at lunch, dinner, everything. If there wasn't a bushel of clams on the porch, we wouldn't eat so good. There are many families that lived off this river during the Depression."

which in turn consumed 10,000 pounds of diatoms and myriad other little creepie crawlies in the sea.

Given its complexity and fragility—this despite its status as a buffer against the power of the sea—the littoral is not an environment immune to the tinkerings of humankind, and in fact suffers the greater when assaulted. Physical damage inflicted on estuarine vegetation by human activities may endure for years, especially if this trauma combines with turbidity caused

by storm runoff and heavy boat traffic. These multiple conditions will prevent sunlight from reaching the submerged plants, inhibiting photosynthesis and reducing replacement through growth. While two or three denuded pathways gouged through an extensive eelgrass bed may not seem the ultimate in environmental calamity, multiply that by the passage of perhaps a hundred boats on any given summer weekend and the result may well be a fragmentation of the habitat to such a degree that it cannot withstand the additional assaults of natural tide and storm action or the incessant pounding of powerboat wakes.

The direct effects of recreational traffic on the estuary can be seen primarily in noticeably turbid water and some degree of physical damage to marine and shoreside vegetation. But considering the small area of the Shark River anchorage and the fact that it berths many more pleasure boats, proportionately, than any other bay on the Jersey coast, its fragile littoral is remarkably intact.

One testament to this is the wonderful variety and the level of activity of the birds that convocate

Green heron. *A surprising number of green herons make the Shark River estuary their home, considering the degree of development that surrounds the bay. These pint-sized relatives of the great blue heron and the American egret nest in low trees and shrubs in the riverine woodlands that exist along the upper estuary. My own observations indicate that about five pairs call Shark River home, and, depending on the tide, the sight of an individual winging its buoyant, bouncy way across the water en route to greener fishing pastures is a common one in summer. In the nineteenth century, this little heron was popularly known as the "fly-up-the-creek."*

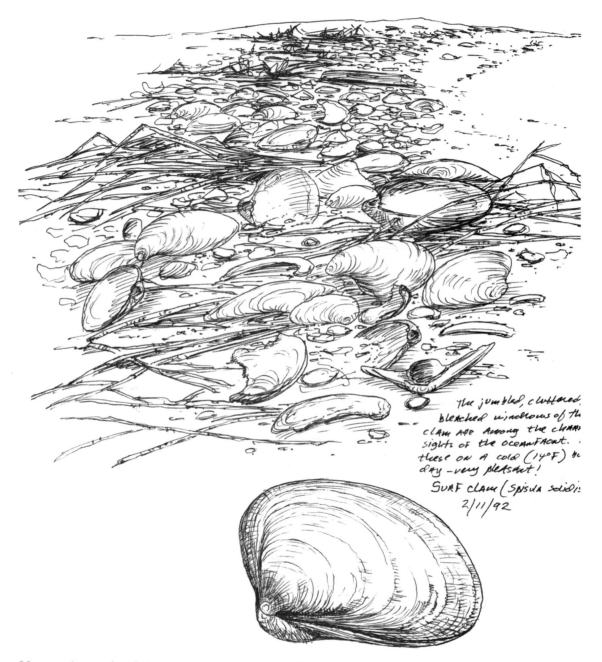

The jumbled, cluttered, bleached windrows of the clam are among the charm sights of the oceanfront. . these on a cold (14°F) day — very pleasant!

Surf clam (Spisula solidis 2/11/92

Vast windrows of surf clams, both empty shells and living animals. *A common sight on the outer beaches all along the Atlantic coast. When freshly stranded, these big, robust clams cannot be opened by gulls since they are too large and heavy to be carried aloft and dropped on the beach; before long, however, they begin to gape, offering the gulls a great gustatory bonanza!*

Mussel territory. *The new tenants of the old Hotel Van Dyke's promenade are those that have little or no appreciation of the bygone dazzle and social shenanigans the venerable "boards" symbolize. Much of the length of the derelict boardwalk along the north shore of the southwest arm of the estuary is buttressed by a still-standing bulkhead about three feet in height. The structure is entirely exposed to air at lower tides but is nonetheless heavily colonized by a wide variety of marine life. One of the more common organisms is the ribbed mussel, a hardy bivalve able to tolerate wide ranges of salinity (and water quality) and extended periods of drying by tidal exposure. Although considered marginally edible, the ribbed mussel cannot hold a candle to the strictly marine blue mussel of worldwide culinary fame.*

Beachcomber souvenir. *In late summer the beaches and tidal flats are often littered with the sun-dried, gull-picked remains of bluefish, the end-of-summer testament to the success of the recreational fishing season. Bluefish skulls and vertebrae can be further dried out and bleached by the beachcomber and rendered into interesting, natural winter conversation pieces, though, like eau de skunk, that oily fish odor never quite departs completely and will often make its presence known to the nostrils on rainy or damp days.*

A pair of horseshoe crabs mating in the clear, shallow waters off the local beach. *If any scene might express the quiet poignancy of species decline, this one does.*

upon the flats, following the cycle of the seasons and the rim of the tide as it rises and falls with the advancing hour. Depending on the time of year, Shark River's tidal flats are a living collage of birds; for the myriad shorebirds of early fall, the fishing herons and egrets of summer, and the ubiquitous gulls of take-your-pick month of the year, the broad, shining flats are quite purely and simply nature's bounteous table laid bare. Here can be found the true "seven-course meal" of the sea, for the largesse of this rich, marginal environment includes a multitude of

Shark River's main boat channel. *From the inlet to the bay, the channel is lined solid with marinas and bulkheads, and many fish species find abundant food and shelter amid the virtual forest of pilings. As I was sitting on a floating dock one morning, just "watching the tide roll away," my eye was caught by a shadowy movement in the water nearby. Leaning over for a closer look, I saw a duo of large orange filefish lazily holding their position against the ebbing tide, seemingly attracted to the meager shelter offered by an algae-festooned rope trailing in the current. The sketching of fish in the natural habitat can be an iffy proposition, given the flighty nature of the beasts, but the slow-moving filefish can be most cooperative subjects if not spooked by sudden movements on the part of the artist.*

The orange file is the largest filefish found along the New Jersey coast, usually appearing inshore during the warmer months. Looking something like an oversized, animated pork chop, this bizarre creature is variously barred and mottled in orange, brown, and white and moves about in such a bumbling, comical manner—even standing on its head at times—that it has earned itself the widespread nickname "foolfish."

algae (dominated by the rumpled sheets of bright green sea lettuce), vast tribes of the seen and unseen marine invertebrates, and numberless fishes that ply the inches-deep waters at the very edge of the land.

Although the density of populations of subterranean invertebrates may vary widely over the total extent of an estuary, it is safe to say that a square yard of tidal flat harbors a virtual zoo of hidden organisms. These range from the near-microscopic diatoms and dinoflagellates that are the dietary mainstay of the animate life of the estuary to countless isopods, tube-, sand-, and lugworms, burrowing anemones, and that well-known group of commercially important creatures, the mollusks.

Shark River is home to roughly ninety species of mollusks (the name is from the Latin, for "soft") in some twelve genera. The great majority of these are small and inconspicuous species seldom observed by the casual littoral explorer reluctant to grope about in the "smud"

A trio of black-backed gulls.

Old swimming float and dock. *The defunct swimming float (upper sketch) was tethered to a stake driven into the ground, ensuring that it didn't simply up and float away at the next high tide. The shores of many coastal estuaries are awash with all manner of wood drift and docks in a tenuous state of togetherness. This flotsam shifts about with every full-moon tide and may even find its way once again out through the inlet and into the open ocean, to come ashore somewhere else and become "somebody else's problem."*

Such a fate would not befall the old dock (lower sketch); it's built of slab concrete with a wooden facing, and although the planks and pilings have seen better days, the core will last for many years to come.

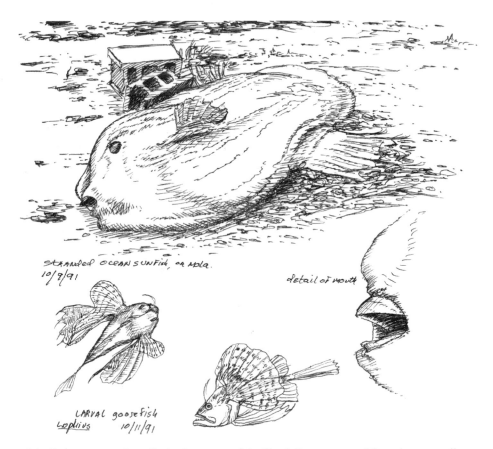

stranded ocean sunfish, or mola.
10/9/91

detail of mouth

LARVAL goosefish
Lophius 10/11/91

Mola and goosefish. *Fishes great and small ply the waters of the Shark River estuary. These drawings illustrate two of the greater and the lesser of marine creatures that may find their way into the estuary from the sea via the inlet—the gargantuan ocean sunfish, or mola, and the larval young of many fish, including this bizarre little goosefish. The sunfish, a vast, grayish creature that looks rather like an animated mattress with fins, washed ashore in late August just south of the Memorial Park beach, where it was discovered by a friend of mine. I visited the site the next day and found that although some deterioration of the great, cartilaginous body had occurred, it was remarkably undamaged. I left in the sketch the rather unattractive cement blocks that were on the beach, for they serve to establish a sense of scale. The animal was about five feet long and weighed an estimated 350 pounds; it had the ominously spongy feel of a great, shark-skinned water bed.*

The flowery, butterflylike creature (below) is the postlarval stage of the amazingly ugly goosefish, better known to supermarket seafood shoppers as monkfish. In the adult, the goosefish is a formidable creature indeed, being about four feet long, up to thirty pounds in weight, and having a huge mouth armed with sharp, very capable teeth. It is strictly a bottom-dwelling predator that will ambush and devour all manner of prey, from smaller fishes to diving birds, but at this stage of its development—just before descending to its sea-bottom existence—the creature is an ephemeral, gauzy, almost transparent scrap of life that drifts about at the mercy of the currents hunting its minute planktonic fare. This one, about three-fourths of an inch long, was netted drifting and tumbling about on the incoming tide; I held it temporarily in a clean mayonnaise jar while I drew it.

Death and life. *Walking the bay beach this brisk, windy October day, I came across a reminder of death in the midst of life in the often harsh littoral environment. I thought this stark, wind- and sun-dried albacore "rack" of skull and backbone presented a stark contrast to the vibrant green of a nearby clump of ordinary crabgrass, the latter hanging on in the sere, sandblasted soil of the upper beach. The late oceanic fish was yet another casualty of the summer's recreational fishing season; the plant, on the other hand, had stubbornly staked its claim. Crabgrass can and will grow virtually anywhere there is even a modicum of soil to nourish its matlike root system. It is one of the hardiest, most universal "weeds" in North America, one of its favorite haunts being the carefully tended suburban lawn.*

of the flats, but a few are large and accessible enough to constitute rather prominent, though low-profile, features of the estuarine habitat. Take the clams, for example. All of the estuary's larger clam (and mussel) species are off-limits to both commercial and recreational harvest at this writing, but a fair number, usually hard-shell (the quahog of New England) clams, are dug for bait by local anglers. The bivalves, owing to their natural vocations as filter feeders, are highly susceptible to waterborne contaminants and toxins, storing them in their tissues and passing the lethal bounty along to the unsuspecting human diner. The prohibitions imposed on clam harvesting in order to head off food poisoning in seafood lovers has been an inadvertent boon to Shark River's bivalves. With the cessation of any significant commercial harvesting, the populations have increased to the point that the demolished remains of clam shells dropped by enterprising herring and ring-billed gulls onto rooftops and roadways are once again a common sight.

An albacore carcass. *This was in a less advanced state of decay and lying in the shallows of the estuary following the powerful nor'easter of late October 1991. The albacore, an oceanic species, seemed much more abundant than usual the summer of that year, with many schools appearing inshore, just off the surf. This beautiful fish is a superbly adapted marine predator, designed for speed and maneuverability in the roughest water. Unlike those of the voracious bluefish, schools of albacore are at once recognized by the acrobatic leaping of the members as they pursue bait fishes right into the surf wash.*

Milar

Early-arriving brant on the beach. *This small party of the attractive, gregarious little "sea geese" was among the scattered first arrivals of the autumn migration that annually brings thousands of brant to Shark River. The gray silences of the midwinter estuary are banished by the joyful din the great flocks give voice to almost constantly, for the brant is a much more conversational bird than its close relative, the Canada goose. Several members of this flock interrupted their meal of sea lettuce to edge closer and closer while I sat drawing them, exhibiting the great curiosity this little goose is known for.*

old bulkheads, still on the job. North cove 10/16/91

DUNE CRICKET

Bulkheads. *The sea effects change, attempts to take hold of the land where it meets the water and shift it, move it somewhere else, usually against the wishes of the people who live there. For this reason, bulkheads and retaining walls were invented. At Shark River, the shoreline is held together with walls, usually of low profile and extending deep into the sand or mud in order to prevent what's behind them from being carried off by wind and wave. One of the simpler bulkhead designs (lower sketch) is just a row of heavy logs lined up along the upper beach, held in place by sawed-off pilings, and faced with planks to contain the sand above. The approach has worked with a fair degree of success, for the cove faces west, away from the sea, and is not often exposed to high winds and tides.*

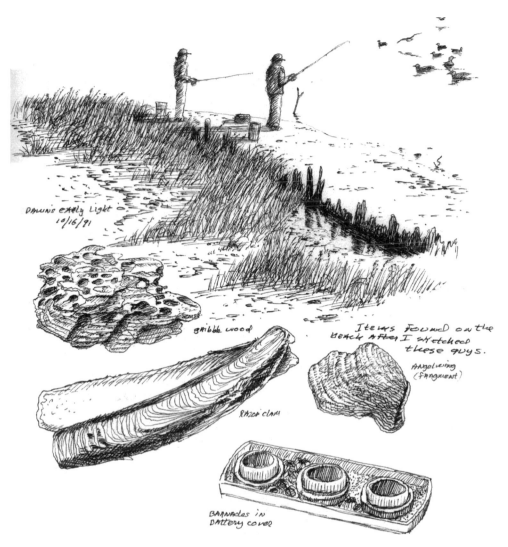

Dawn's Early Light.
10/16/91

gribble wood

Items found on the beach after I sketched these guys.

Angelwing (fragment)

Razor clam

Barnacles in battery cover

Early-morning flounder fishing. *Well into the fall season, the "bennies" of summer have long since departed and the estuary is flat, its surface unscarred by the wakes of powerboats and jetskis. Mornings are chill and bright, the light of the fall sun soft and evanescent, and the first of the winter flounder, or black-backs, begin the yearly trek inshore. On such mornings, along about 7:30, guys on their way to work or a few retirees with time to kill may be seen wetting a line along the shore, hoping for that early flounder. I used to try my hand at it as well, but it was always something of a problem stashing the fish (if I was successful) in the office fridge among the brown-bag lunches of my colleagues.*

These days, I prowl the early-morning flats in search of "artifacts" presented me by the arriving or departing tides. Few of my finds would make a museum curator tremble with excitement, but such modest little treasures as this intricate bit of "gribble wood," the angelwing shell, or the big razor clam, provide a pleasant kickoff to what would be "just another day at the office."

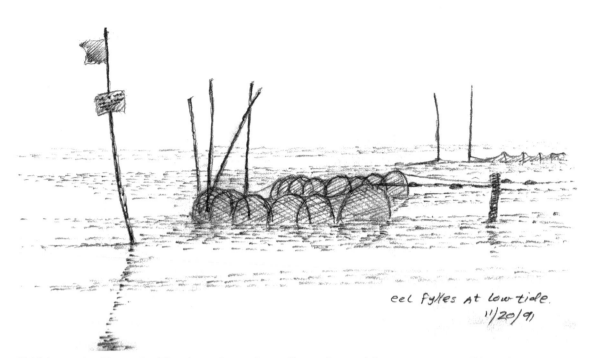

eel fykes at low tide.
11/20/91

Eel fykes at dead low tide. *This shows the simple yet effective design of this ancient, passive fishing device: a series of large hoops containing a progression of smaller and smaller net funnels that direct the eels into the containment chamber at the end. Fykes are tended by their operators every twelve to twenty-four hours, the time interval depending on the season of the year.*

The basic life-style of clams dictates that they are inextricably tied to the substrate when it comes to living quarters, though they are by no means totally immobile there. Although considered by most people to be formless lumps of seemingly randomly assembled tissue neatly packaged in a nondescript shell and capable of little in the way of social interaction, clams and other bivalves are in reality far from the crashing bores they've been made out to be.

Nobody knows for sure just where the phrase "happy as a clam" originated, but one would suspect that it had something to do with the animal's life-style. After all, a clam's life wouldn't appear to be one of vast complexity, consisting primarily of respirating, eating, and engaging in molluscan sex— all from within the confines of that sturdy and inviolate shell.

But though clams, through the very nature of their anatomy, would indeed appear to be the ultimate in sedentary

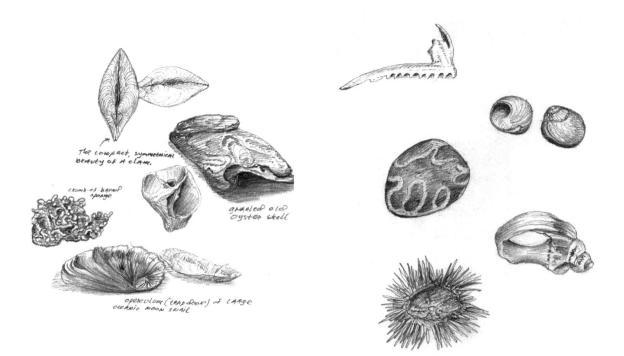

Bits and pieces of the beach. Top to bottom: *The compact symmetry of a clam is seen in this live macoma clam picked up on the beach; this ancient oyster shell shows its accumulated years in the many layers of shell growth and its overall thickness— about an inch at the heel of the shell; weatherworn whelk shell; crumb-of-bread sponge; the thin, flat operculum of a large moon snail.*

living among nature's creatures, they do get around, after their own fashion and in their own good time. Bivalves occupy many submarine habitats other than the conventional mudflats; they are found everywhere in both saline and, in declining numbers, freshwater environments. Whether the place be the lightless, abyssal depths of the sea or the warm, shallow littoral, there is a

Bits and pieces of the beach. Top to bottom: *A bluefish jaw, sans teeth (in this old, wave-worn bone, the dentures have fallen out, leaving behind the conspicuous, empty sockets); two views of the common periwinkle shell; a curious, marbled shale rock; whelk shell worn away to the point that it is a mere ring of shell; a purple sea urchin that has been picked clean by gulls.*

clam, scallop, or mussel species in tenacious residence there.

To get technical about it, clams are members of the phylum Mollusca, the class Pelecypoda, the order Eulamellicbranchia, and the families Veneridae, Myacidae, and Solenidae— all three families containing species in high standing as seafood in the Shark River area. Clams are, for the most part,

Hotdoggin' it on the river (above and right). *The jetski, or "personal watercraft," has become a much more visible, and audible, presence at Shark River over the past ten years. Responsibly operated, the jetski is nothing more than a noisy distraction to those seeking the peace and quiet of the natural shore experience; however, indifference and selfishness on the part of a few operators quickly transform the machine into an environmental liability of the first magnitude. Damage to fragile shallow-water habitats and harassment of wildlife are two of the more serious charges lodged against irresponsible jetski use, with posing a hazard to boat navigation a close third.*

I was able to work up these drawings by asking a couple of hotdoggers if they'd mind spinning a few tight turns close to the beach. They readily obliged.

classically sedentary animals, though a few, such as the tasty razor clam, can effect some pretty swift evasive action in the avoidance of capture. Bivalves— edible ones, that is—are tonged, pitchforked, raked, "noodled" for by toe, or grabbed by hand for table use. Whatever the technique employed, the activity is generally referred to as, logically enough, "clamming."

Of late, clamming has become something of an endangered occupation in the Shark River estuary as well as elsewhere along the Middle Atlantic coast. Owing to the combined factors of water pollution and overharvesting, the catch has declined considerably over the past twenty years, and a host of often complex shellfish regulations have emerged. The result is a decided loss of simplicity for clammers, for no longer can a bushel of hard-shells be dug for the table with innocent abandon, and certainly not with

The Riverside Drive beach. *A favorite launching spot for boaters, anglers, and jetskiers.*

impunity. The once bucolic activity, like many other environment-oriented recreational pursuits in this day and age, has acquired the status of a regulated occupation, with all the attendant rules and red tape.

But clamming regulations exist for two principal reasons. First, shellfish are an edible and thus a valuable resource, and since virtually all clam beds lie within the jurisdiction of a town or other such political entity, somebody, somewhere, expects you to pay for the privilege of digging your own seafood. Even though the land is regularly submerged under tidal waters, it is owned by someone or is under the control of a local government.

The second reason concerns the matter of health. Marine pollution has become more than a minor annoyance along much of the Middle Atlantic seaboard, and people who eat bivalves taken from contaminated areas generally get sick—uncomfortably, inconveniently, and often very painfully so. Today, more than a quarter of the total New Jersey clam habitat is closed due to pollution, and that figure is not likely to decline in the near future. It is currently against the law to harvest shellfish directly for consumption from all Monmouth County coastal waters as well as those of northern Ocean County. Perhaps more ominously, the ban extends to all ocean waters within three miles of the coast!

The standard warning posted by the New Jersey Department of Environmental Protection indicating that a particular clamming area has been closed to harvesting consists of the familiar bright red circle with the diagonal line, this drawn through figures representing hard and soft clams, an oyster, and a blue mussel. All Shark River tidal flats are off-limits to both recreational and commercial harvest at this writing, and the presence of the posted signs on a shoreline generally means that the flats beyond are under a

Black-backed gulls and plastic owls lining up on the pilings at one of the marinas. *The counterfeit owls are often pressed into service to discourage such avian pests as pigeons and starlings from roosting or nesting on structures and subsequently fouling them with their highly acidic droppings. Around marinas, gulls are regarded in much the same way—as creatures somewhat less than picturesque—by both marina operators and boatowners, hence the presence of the plastic "scare-gulls" on the pilings. As can be readily seen here, they are almost laughingly ineffective. Two other, much simpler approaches—driving several large spikes into the piling tops or milling them into a pointed cone shape—effectively discourage all but the most persistent of the avian loiterers.*

BRANT gathering to DRINK AT A
team DRAIN STREAM ON the MUDFLAT.
12/2.W

Brant at storm drain. *At low tide the runoff from one of the street drains meanders across the mudflat like some sort of tiny coastal river. The wintering brant are attracted to this dubious source of drinking water, and throughout the day scattered flocks can be seen and heard as they gather at the popular watering spot for a slug of "Neptune City gin." Few sickly or dead brant ever turn up on Shark River's winter beaches, so it must be assumed that whatever chemical delights may be carried to the estuary through the drain runoff, they have little or no effect on the cast-iron lower GI of a brant!*

The "hot seat." I used this
makeshift Fishermens' chair
to sketch the scene above.

Recycled artifact. *Exactly how a 1960s-style dining room chair found its way to a Shark River beach is anybody's guess, but even though it has been reduced to nothing more than a rusted frame, its life of service to humanity is not yet ended; seated with a weathered length of planking, it makes a perfectly serviceable perch from which to fish for fluke or eels, or to sketch the scene unfolding off the beach. In the case of this particular artist, it was the crowd of brant gathering in noisy camaraderie at the street drain rivulet, shown in the preceding drawing.*

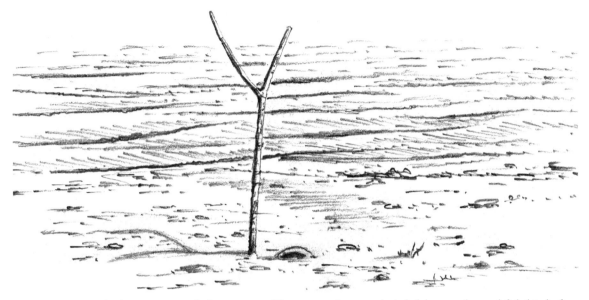

Still life. *A twig, looking very out-of-place on a mudflat, is in reality a makeshift fishing-rod prop left behind after a day's angling.*

"blanket prohibition." In other words, if a game warden catches you with a handful of fat hard-shells on a posted flat, it won't do you any good to plead that you were collecting them for bait. On a closed flat, no clamming means just that; the fish cops reason, probably rightly so, that leaving a "bait digging" loophole in the law would allow a disreputable clammer to sneak the critters off the flats a few at a time over a few days, give them a cursory rinse, and peddle them to the local eatery.

But in spite of the extensive clam bed closures and the risk involved in dining on bivalves harvested anywhere in the Northeast, the New Jersey Bureau of Shellfisheries annually issues about thirteen thousand recreational and two thousand commercial permits.

In Shark River, clamming regulations are little more than a moot point, for the entire estuary is presently closed to clamming even though hard-shell and soft-shell clams are now quite abundant here, and for the obvious reason. The shellfish beds are usually closed when the so-called *E. coli* count consistently rises to more than seventy per 100 milliliters of water. By contrast, areas certified for public swimming may have periodic counts as high as 100 coliform bacteria per 100 milliliters.

12:30 pm, Low tide. Brant and gulls gather... the seasonal bay bottom

Low tide. *A time of bird sounds and sea smells, the wind and sun and the refreshing, eternal cycle of the sea.*

Escherichia coli is one of Shark River's less than desirable aquatic invertebrates, but it is vitally important as the bellwether of disease-causing pollution. The bacteria, present naturally in the large intestine of all warm-blooded animals, including humans, in itself and in moderate numbers is no threat to life and limb.

Straight marine water is not favorable to the production of the bacteria and thus high densities are inhibited in the sea, but the estuarine situation, with its lower salinities and numerous nonpoint (nonspecific) sources of pollution—the haunt of most of our edible mollusks—is perfectly suited to *E. coli* and thus the danger of bivalves picking up great numbers of them is much higher there.

Another organic toxic threat is paralytic shellfish poisoning, or PSP, in which a single-celled alga generates a toxin harmful to warm-blooded animals. The culprit here is *Gonyaulax tamarensis*, an organism considered halfway between a plant and an animal in that it is capable of propelling itself about through the use of minute flagellae yet photosynthesizes its nourishment from sunlight like a true plant. These delightful little creatures produce a natural toxin that accumulates in the tissues of the bivalves that filter them in vast numbers from the water column; the poison attacks the central nervous system of the unwary human clam lover with potentially dangerous ferocity.

But all these dire dietary rumblings aside, left to themselves bivalves are harmless, intriguing creatures. All are filter feeders, drawing food-bearing water across their gills through ciliary (waving) action, separating the wheat from the chaff, and delivering the edible to the gut. They must have moving, circulating water to replenish their oxygen supply, bring food to them, and carry away waste matter. Suspended heavy metals and other contaminants are accepted by the feeding clam right along with all the usual diatoms and flagellates, hence the special danger attached to eating any filter feeders found in polluted environments.

Most bivalves are capable of some degree of motion, the popular conception notwithstanding, though this varies widely according to the

Old wood bulkhead,
SHARK River Inlet
June 18th '91

Restraints on the sea. *The inlet itself is given some semblance of permanence in the face of the power of the sea by an often jumbled but somehow ordered arrangement of jetties, T-groins, and wooden bulkheads. In the conventional maritime engineering wisdom, such constructions inhibit the lateral (up and down the coast) movement of sand by inshore currents and storm tides, and prevent the inlet from gradually filling with silt and becoming a delta, a feat it is eternally attempting to accomplish. The jetties are successful to a degree, except for the fact that those beaches on the south side tend to gain sand and widen, while those on the north lose it, much to the dismay of many shore towns and landowners.*

This bulkhead is only about thirty years old yet already shows signs of corrosion and deterioration. On the day I drew it, a small group of late-migrating purple sandpipers and a greater yellowlegs were on the scene.

rockweed (Fucus) --
rotted dock piling

ring billed gulls
preening this species
is second in abundance
to the herring gull. The
laughing and black-back
gulls round out the estuary's
gull roster in summers.
6/18/91

Ring-billed gull. *This gull differs from the much more coastal herring, black-back, and laughing gulls in that it is quite cosmopolitan in nature, being found far from the sea and in a wide variety of situations, from river valleys to farmers' fields and parking lots of shopping malls. The ring-bill is usually quite fearless and displays a good deal more savvy than most gulls, which as a group are far from lacking in that quality. While the larger black-backed and herring gulls are somewhat wary and seldom allow a close approach, the ring-bill and the laughing varieties will crowd right up to people cleaning fish or engaging in any other activity that promises scraps of edibles. These birds were attending to their toilet on pilings not ten feet distant and for the most part ignored me as I sketched them preening.*

Also illustrated (right) is the ultimate fate of the average piling—most are sunk too deeply to be easily pulled during dock repairs, so they are simply left in place to slowly erode and rot into the sand or mud. The end result is a virtual nub of wood covered with barnacles and tiny mussels and festooned with kelp. This one was located just below the high-tide mark, and even when high and dry, its garlands of rockweed harbored a virtual zoo of tiny isopods and mysid shrimp seeking shelter from the blazing summer sun until the next tide ransomed them.

Laughing gull studies
venus drawing AB

The ebullient laughing gull. *More so than the larger and heavier herring and black-back gulls, this gull is the epitome of buoyant grace and indefatigable curiosity. A trim, attractively patterned gull, the "laugher" is the principal "voice" of the summer seashore, its strident, spirited calls, sounding very much like the human expression of joyful mirth, ring far and wide, especially above the birds' crowded nesting colonies.*

The laughing gull exhibits a bold and fearless personality and is one of the more prominent avian "hangers on" around docks and marinas, always on the lookout for a free meal. Although enterprising, it does not engage in the "clam dropping" tactics employed by the larger herring gull to open live bivalves.

I caught a group of laughing gulls on one of the estuary's bathing beaches, where their ceaseless activity gave me the opportunity to execute some good, varied field studies of the birds. In my opinion, there are few more attractive seabirds than this lovely, albeit noisy, creature.

Laughing gulls on old dock supports. *This species is one of the more common gulls in the New Jersey shore area; it is highly visible, and audible, and can be quite tame and fearless around docks where fish are being gutted and cleaned by successful anglers. I sketched these birds from a nearby beach, the major problem being that over the course of the production of the drawing, several different individuals came and went in rapid succession. As a result, I had to very quickly rough in the form of a bird as it landed and finish the figure later. The wood pilings were more cooperative subjects and thus were drawn in more detail in one "sitting."*

species. Oysters and mussels are true stay-at-homes, permanently anchored to a solid substrate or to one another by strong byssal threads secreted by the living animal. The stolid and heavy surf clam can burrow out of sight within about five minutes by slowly inserting its muscular foot deep into the sand and pulling the shell down behind it. This methodical action is strictly slow motion when compared with the literally fleet-footed razor clam, a molluscan speedster that can zip down its burrow within a second or two.

Shark River's four largest and best-known clam species are all the target, in contaminant-free waters, of commercial clammers and are highly popular with seafood lovers. Starting with the surf, or ocean clam, the biggest of all, they are:

• The surf clam (*Spisula solidissima*). Also called the sea clam, this animal may reach the length of seven inches across the shell. These clams often litter the beaches in great numbers and are a favorite seashore artifact of beachcombing kids and adults who favor natural ash trays. Surf clams, contrary to the name, occur not only in the surf zone but far offshore where they are dredged in a sizable commercial fishery that supplies the bait and chowder markets.

• The hard-shell clam (*Mercenaria mercenaria*). Known as the quahog (pronounced "ko-hawg"), littleneck, or cherrystone clam, this animal is doubtless the best-known and most popular edible bivalve. It is the archtypal clam to most people. Its most characteristic field marks are the stout, strongly ridged, grayish shell and the

Double-crested cormorants at the boat anchorage. *Ten years ago, cormorants were quite rare up and down the East Coast and were being considered for federal classification as Endangered. The birds have since increased greatly in number, owing to protection from persecution by commercial fishermen and to the cessation of the use of the insecticide DDT. These rangy "sea crows" are common in Shark River during the winter and spring months, where they seem to favor the sheltered "backwaters" of boatyards and anchorages. They are a common sight perched on anchor buoys, wings outstretched in the familiar "American eagle" pose to dry in the sun and wind.*

These big, black birds can be elusive sketch subjects, for they constantly dive or sink slowly out of sight in search of fish, but since they tend to stick to a generally small area of water, the artist is afforded plenty of opportunity to work up a composite sketch as a bird repeatedly reappears on the surface.

The handwritten notes in the illustration read:

Ruddy turnstones picking stranded mussels on beach.

Dunlin

A few studies of August shorebirds moving through the Shark River estuary. Most of these individuals were adults in the late summer transition between breeding and winter plumages.

Sunday, August 4

early-migrating purple sandpipers on jetty

Royal tern

Shark River shorebird vignettes. *Shown is a potpourri of coastal birds I observed and sketched at the Shark River environs on a very hot, hazy, and humid day at the Jersey shore. August marks the beginning of the fall shorebird migration along the Atlantic Coast, and the estuary and nearby oceanfront attract good numbers of avian wayfarers heading south.*

I drew the ruddy turnstones, purple sandpipers, and black-bellied plovers at the ocean beach, where they either rested in the course of the journey or probed the sea wrack at the high-tide line. Great numbers of blue mussels had been washed ashore by a recent storm tide, and the turnstones, in particular, were attracted to this windfall, energetically probing and flipping over the mass of gaping bivalves and eating the exposed meat. The impressive royal tern was one of a pair that was winging up and down the shoreline near Oliver's Marina. This species is an irregular visitor to the estuary, breeding farther south along the coast, but whenever it appears it presents an immediate and striking contrast to the much smaller and more graceful common, roseate, and Forster's terns most commonly associated with the New Jersey shore environment. This bird proved to be a cooperative model, frequently returning to alight on a nearby piling and staying put for minutes at a time.

Bottlehead
Buffies are very common and "All over the place", flying swiftly back and forth.

Greater Scaup
This species occurs in limited numbers in winter. 30~50 birds on a given day would be about average.

Waterfowl. *These are very much an integral part of the Shark River scene at all times of the year, but especially so during the colder months. These drawings, made in mid-April, show two species—the bufflehead and greater scaup—that are fairly abundant in the estuary, and one, the surf scoter, that is found primarily on the open ocean. Ducks can be cooperative subjects and at the same time rather frustrating. When resting or feeding, most species remain "in position" long enough for the artist to get at least a rough outline of pattern and form, but in most environments, waterfowl are quite wary and seldom allow a close approach. The artist, thus, must be content with squinting at distant, ducklike specks on the wing or water, or peering through binoculars for intermittent close-up looks at the subjects.*

Bay ducks wintering at Shark River, such as the little buffie and the scaup, or bluebill, are quite accustomed to people, and since the area is off-limits to hunting of any kind, both species can be approached closely enough for good, detailed sketching.

SNOWY EGAETS AT DAWN
10/9/91

engine trouble

Snowy egrets and stalled lobstermen. *As the sun lifts from the sea and hangs just above the eastern shore of the bay, little actions catch the eye. A pair of egrets come into view; they seem extensions of the sunken spar they've spent the night on. Only small, quick motions of their heads betray them; the birds seek the first signs of the fish of their day's work. Nearby, shadows move across the deck of a small lobsterman dead in the water. Muffled, reproachful voices drift across the water. Engine trouble, delaying the impending labors of the hard-pressed fishermen.*

I found that the drawing of the lobstermen was best executed very broadly in permanent marker, for the boat and men were directly in front of the rising sun and in deep shadow and thus no details were visible.

The baldpate, or American wigeon. *One of the commoner winter ducks of the estuary, these remain abundant in recent years while other species, such as the canvasback and pintail, have declined in number. Wigeon gather in sizable flocks in Musquash Cove, pretty much shunning the wider areas of the bay. At lower tides they dabble and probe the mud, eating a wide variety of organic fare, with the bright green alga known as sea lettuce a special favorite. For some reason, baldpate flocks are composed mostly of the strikingly colored males; they outnumber the females by about five to one.*

The solitary sandpiper. *This species is well named, for only rarely have I seen such birds gathered in even small groups. These odd, almost "contemplative" little shorebirds are usually observed solemnly and deliberately patrolling the shoreline.*

soft purple wash of color on the inside of the valves. A hard-shell two inches across is called the cherrystone, after Virginia's Cherrystone Inlet.

This clam was relished by the coastal Indians who actively harvested it for food; the shell was fashioned into ornaments and used as currency in the form of wampum. The hard-shell clam is the species most often dug from the sand by gulls and dropped on the roadways to access the meat inside.

• The soft-shell clam (*Mya arenaria*). The famous steamer, gaper, or "piss clam" is a common animal in Shark River, despite the activities of sandworm diggers and other pokers and

A mallard and her brood patrolling the edges of weed beds on the upper river. *This species is the primary breeding duck of the estuary, followed by the closely related black duck. Mallard hens may be seen escorting their broods in a wide variety of settings, from the more conventional wooded upper river through the brackish marshes of the estuary to the oceanfront beaches. Mortality among ducklings is rather high here and is due, for the most part, to the depredations of snapping turtles and the large population of resident and distinctly predatory herring and black-backed gulls.*

prodders of the mudflats, human or beast. Stomp on the soft ground, and the local soft-shells will give themselves away with the characteristic squirts that have earned them their New Jersey nickname. The shell is oblongish in shape, rather thin in construction, and a chalky white in a rinsed animal. Unlike the hard-shell, this clam cannot retract completely inside a tightly closed shell. Usually raked or forked from the mudflats, soft-shell clams should be held in clean water for about three hours so they can purge themselves of sand and other debris.

Care should be taken in harvesting these clams, for their shells are rather fragile and will break with rough handling. Soft-shells are normally steamed. The meat is wonderful, dipped in drawn butter, and the broth is superb!

1/16/92

Winter feeding activities of large, mixed flocks of brant and bufflehead. *The little buffies seem particularly attracted to the brant flocks and consort with them in seeming harmony—more so than any other waterfowl species. The bufflehead is a deep diver that hunts crustaceans down on the cold, dark bay bottom. The American wigeon also shadows the brant as they feed in shallow water, but for the purpose of pirating the succulent sea lettuce the little sea geese feed on; they will adroitly snatch the marine greenery from the goose's bill as the hardworking victim brings it up from the bottom.*

• Common and short razor clams (*Ensis directus* and *Ensis tagulus*). One of the best-tasting clams, the athletic common razor clam, or jackknife clam, is rarely consumed raw, but rather fried or steamed. The razor clam can move fast when it has to; when it senses danger it thrusts its elongated, muscular foot deep into its burrow, expands the tip, and pulls itself downward with a swift and powerful contraction. The clam can often "outrun" a single digger, so it's best to hunt it in pairs—one person to drive a spade beside the burrow and compress the mud with a hard pull on the handle, while the other hurriedly digs the critter out.

The shell of a clam, in particular the rugged, tight-fitting valves of the hard-shell clam, serves its owner well as a fortress against the culinary designs of a hostile world. A clam, after all, is little more than a collection of soft, tender, and very vulnerable internal organs wearing its skeleton on the outside. But as unappetizing as the exposed anatomy of the bivalve may appear to the unappreciative eye, the taste of a shucked clam has an almost magical appeal to a wide variety of creatures, not in the least excluding walruses, nearly all gulls, and human gourmets who scarf down raw quahogs with an expression of ecstasy on their faces.

The gadwall, or "gray duck." *This species is present at Shark River in small numbers year-round. Because I have never seen females with young, I suspect it hasn't found suitable nesting habitat here and thus is present in summer only as a nonbreeder.*

Confronted with a tightly closed hard-shell or surf clam, both gulls and humans have over the ages devised ways to open it, both of them logical, and both effective. If the clam is small enough to be carried, the gull takes it aloft and drops it on a hard surface, shattering the shell and exposing the bounty within. This seemingly ingenious behavior (for a gull) is apparently learned and not inherited, for older gulls are far more adept at it than first- and second-year birds. Young birds have particular trouble in determining just what constitutes a hard surface, and with the accurate gauging of two critical distances: the height to which the clam must be carried to break it, and the proximity of other gulls, which are marvelously adept at seafood piracy. I once watched a callow, first-year herring gull at Memorial Park repeatedly drop a hefty hard-shell clam from a great height while its flock-fellows on the beach below watched the action with interest but made no move to steal the bivalve. The reason: the inexperienced bird, believing that any flat surface would suffice as a clam-anvil, was dropping the creature in water only a few inches deep just off the beach. To no avail, of course, and the older and wiser birds simply stood by and watched with what turned out

A dense crowd of American brant on the flat waters of the sheltered "back side" of the estuary. *Brant, the smallest North American goose, has made an encouraging recovery over the past twenty-five years following a sharp decline after its principal food plant, eelgrass, was nearly wiped out by a viral disease in the 1930s. This noisy, active flock was feeding on Ulva, or sea lettuce, which brant have learned to accept as a reasonable substitute food on their wintering grounds. This adaptability ultimately saved the species from extinction.*

In the Shark River estuary, brant are accustomed to the close-proximity humans (no gunning is permitted anywhere in the estuary); thus I was able to approach this flock quite closely and draw the birds from the beach. I used an HB hard carbon pencil and, since there was so much motion and activity, simply made an attempt to suggest the forms of the more distant birds while trying for more detail in those figures in the foreground.

The wet and reflective effect of water was rather easily attained simply by studying the mirror images cast by any solid and standing objects in the water, in this case, the reeds and old stakes, and quickly and loosely sketching them in. Take careful note of the angle and position of the reflecting objects and be sure to render a "mirror image" as closely as possible, and the reflection effect is in the bag.

A young herring gull. *Most gulls will allow a fairly close approach and, because they will often "hold a pose" for extended periods, are among the easier seashore birds to sketch. The artist looking for an abundance of "seagull" subjects has only to visit a beach, marina, or fishing dock, equipped with pad, pencils, and a loaf of stale bread to attract and hold the birds in the immediate area.*

The American brant—the preeminent, high-profile winter waterfowl of the Shark River estuary. *Two or three thousand of the small geese winter here, and though that number may not seem overly large, when taken in context with the area of the estuary—less than two square miles—it means a water body crowded with a dense gaggle of noisy, active brant. Owing to the absence of boat traffic through the winter months, the brant are able to spend their winter respite in peace. The birds will often remain close by when one wanders the beaches in search of subject material for drawing.*

Brant are easy to
lure close in - simply sit on
the beach and ignore them
and their natural curiosity
does the rest. If a person
conveys no threat, the birds
are very tame and fearless.

detail of head

winter Ruddy Ducks

they typically gather in
compact, dozing flocks on
quieter waters on the bay.

detail of head
Adult Female

The perky, pint-sized ruddy duck. *Although this species has declined in number over the past ten years, many ruddy ducks can still be seen on the estuary, where they gather in tight little flocks in quiet coves. At Shark River, ruddies appear to feed mostly in the early-morning and evening hours, spending much of the day drifting easily on the tide in dozing flocks. These gatherings are interesting in that the flock members seem to have an almost mystical ability to maintain a precise distance from each other. Thus a crowd of snoozing ruddies appears as a regularly distributed bunch of brownish humps on the water, all leisurely twirling in place and bobbing on the gentle swells. Ruddies are oddly loathe to fly when disturbed, preferring to simply sink from sight and swim out of harm's way beneath the surface; when they do take to the air, they have a swift, direct, bumblebeelike flight, the speed of which is accentuated by their small size.*

Grebes. *Roughly a dozen of these odd, secretive little grebes winter on the estuary each year. These almost always appear as solitary little swimmers, each patrolling its own section of bay, usually among the docks and pilings of the more developed waterfront. Pied-bills normally dive in the conventional manner, that is, with a swift upward arc and downward thrust, but at times they simply sink out of sight with nary a ripple, a maneuver that has earned them the nicknames "waterwitch" and "helldiver."*

to be a feigned disinterest as the nonplussed juvenile rose higher and higher with each drop, landed quickly, disgustedly inspected the very much intact clam, picked it up, and began the arduous maneuver all over again.

In due course and seemingly by chance, the frustrated gull discovered the nearby hardpan of the beach; rising to an astronomical height, it airmailed its cargo once again, and this time the clam landed with the telltale "thok!" of success. But alas, the would-be diner had miscalculated both those vital distances, for in the time it took the neophyte clam dropper to descend from that dizzying height to claim its meal,

several of the alert watchers below had made off with the prize.

The gulls' methods are effective but messy. The birds don't mind that at all, but most people would object to picking shards of clamshell out of a meal so we bypass the clam's defenses in a more genteel way, usually referred to as "shucking." If you're new to the art, it would be the better part of prudence to wear work gloves when handling the clams and the requisite knife. This latter should ideally be on the dull side and have a rounded, not pointed, tip. Hold the clam in your strongest hand with the hinged end of the shell in the heel of your hand. With the other hand, wedge the knife blade in the slot between the valves, grip the blade, and "pull" it into the slot, rocking the blade while exerting a steady pressure. The hand that holds the knife does not apply any pressure, but rather only serves to keep it aligned until the adductor muscles are reached and severed, levering the clam open.

A clam's life may indeed be considered an uneventful one on a day-to-day basis, but it's not neccesarily an easy one. A great host of predators and parasites, not to mention natural disasters, may spell doom for the average quahog at any time in its perilous life. Voracious dog whelks and starfish breach the shell of the tasty creature through drilling and muscle power; storm surges unearth it and leave it exposed to the attentions of the gulls; abrupt changes in salinity and water temperature in the estuary may weaken the clam or kill the animal outright.

But by whatever means or method a bivalve meets its inevitable end, it leaves behind hard evidence of its passage through life and time in its empty and rather forlorn valves, which are cast in abundance upon the broad face of the ocean beach. These eroded and ridged remains, among the most

detail of head

StARLings noisily discuss events from a dock edge. These are Among the most Abundant birds of the seashore, sad to say!

Starlings, in evidence, all around the bay. *They find ample provender among the leavings of anglers and the contents of trash cans. As in most other urbanized settings,* Sturnus vulgaris *is often the most abundant and visible bird on the premises.*

familiar objects of the seashore state of mind, manage to maintain their hinged juncture for a time, are then torn asunder by the relentless power of the sea and finally cast upon the shore, to be rolled and pulverized and polished by the surf. In time, the clam's self-made monument to its existence will have been broken and divided again and again and rendered into a thousand minute fragments, each a tiny fraction of the whole, and then reincorporated into the foundations of the earth itself.

The mute swan, a regal but highly aggressive bird. *This swan is much more common along the New Jersey shore today than in the past. It is absolutely fearless when protecting its eggs or young and will unhesitatingly attack a human or beast if threatened. Swans have been known to kill smaller waterfowl that unwittingly intruded on their nesting territories. This mated pair is engaged in leisurely feeding along the high tide shoreline near the Tucker's Point Bridge.*

Part III

Midafternoon; the Salt Marsh; Crabs

The active, aggressive, incredibly feisty blue crab—king of Shark River's crustacean denizens. *The adult blueclaw is an agile hunter of just about any animal it can catch and overpower, and it is not above eating any carrion it comes across in its travels. The larvae, or megalops (upper drawing), is by contrast a macroscopic pelagic wanderer, drifting about according to the whim of the currents and snaring whatever tiny animals come within reach. In spite of an intense recreational and commercial fishery and pollution of its coastal habitats, the bluecrab has, so far, managed to hold its own. It is especially abundant about docks and marinas where fish catches are gutted and cleaned and the refuse tossed to the tide.*

The salt marsh has its genesis in a mudflat. The river delivers its load of sediments, gradually filling the estuary; small channels and creeks thread their complex pathways through the mud to the open water of the bay itself. Salt-tolerant plants colonize the flats, creating in their tangled complexity the support for the further gathering of debris, the life-giving shelter for the myriad creatures that the sea will bring in to begin life in all its marvelous, littorine abundance there.

At one time, the salt and brackish marshes stretched for more than 3,700 lush, green miles along the Atlantic and Gulf coasts of North America; today, they are much reduced in area, and the unique habitat is very much an endangered one.

Volumes have been written, most of them within the past twenty-five years, on the crucial importance of the salt marsh environment. This unique habitat's effect on the warp and weave of the natural world and its vast food chain is complex, profound, and critical. Without the sheltered, nutrient-rich havens offered by the broad fields of sun and grass of the coastal marshes, many, if not most, of the sea's more eminent (and edible) creatures would not have their place of genesis. The young of the great majority of marine fish, great and small, come of age in the benign and nurturing waters of the estuaries, among the aquatic "great plains" of spartina, three-corner rush, and a dozen species of sedge. Without the "worthless swamps" that lie at the edge of the sea, there would be no striped bass, no fluke or flounder, no cod, mackerel, tuna, kingfish, and a host of other oceanic life forms.

The salt-marsh environment is one of the richest on earth. It is estimated that a single acre of salt marsh will produce ten tons of organic matter per year, far outstripping the most productive wheat field, an acre of which will yield but one and a half tons per year, including leaves and stems. A healthy salt marsh will produce about five tons of bottom debris alone, which serves as the crucial nurturing agent for the microscopic mollusks and crustacea that are the principal nourishment of young fishes, that part of the food chain that most interests humans.

Today, the conventional wisdom of free enterprise's officialdom rather

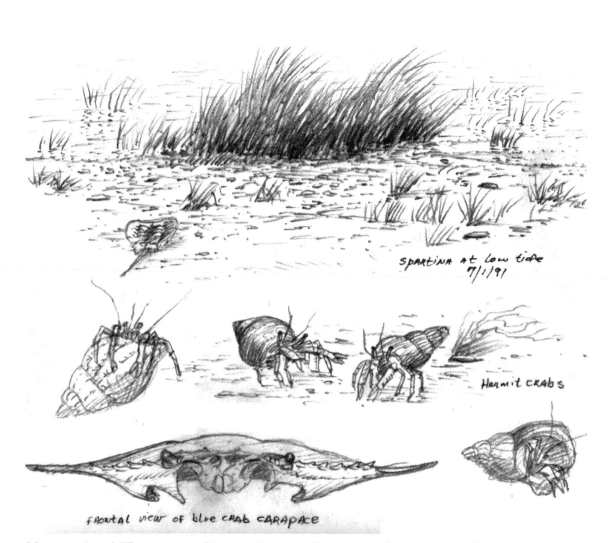

spartina at low tide 7/1/91

Hermit crabs

frontal view of blue crab carapace

Hermit crab turf. *The scene pictured* (upper drawing) *illustrates one of my own personal favorites among marine habitats.*

The sand and mud spartina flat is the home of the spunky, comical little hermit crab, and in favorable areas, hundreds of these little crustaceans may be seen scuttling over the bottom in water only a few inches deep. This is the scene of ceaseless, often frenetic activity. The animals are highly aggressive and active patrollers of the substrate, and when two crabs meet in their rounds there is almost always a brief but spirited skirmish as the pugnacious little creatures size each other up and get into aquatic shoving matches. Although primarily carnivorous, hermits will eat algae and other plants when available, and intently investigate virtually any object of interest.

The major problem confronting a hermit crab as it grows is that of how and where to locate a replacement empty snail shell once it has outgrown its current home. The search is crucial, for without its second-hand armor, the hermit is completely defenseless against predators, of which there are many in the marine environment. Usually, a house-hunting crab will luck out and find an untenanted snail shell, but if things get desperate it will try to oust another hermit from its own shell; the resulting lilliputian combat is understandably of a ferocious nature!

The salt marsh, one of the richest, most productive natural habitats on earth. *These marshes are the aquatic nursery for a great host of fish species and the source of food and shelter for countless other creatures, great and small. The loss of coastal wetlands in this country has been great over the past 100 years, and the Shark River estuary has not escaped that fate. The bay has been extensively dredged in the past, and some of the wetlands have been filled for housing and marina construction; however, the area of surviving salt marsh here is surprisingly large. Most is concentrated in rather broad bands at the mouth of the Shark River itself on the upper estuary.*

At opposite ends of the salt-marsh food chain are the black duck and Ulva, a common summer alga that often carpets the muddy bottom of the more shallow, open areas in bright green cellophanelike masses. This alga, commonly called "sea lettuce," usually attaches itself to a solid object on the substrate by means of a specialized "holdfast," but it is often dislodged by strong currents and tides and drifts free in papery, ripply sheets as long as six feet. Ulva has only moderate food value to aquatic organisms, but it is avidly eaten by black ducks, wigeon, and the small coastal goose, the American brant. I caught this small group of blacks "tipping up" for the plant in the low-tide shallows; they appeared to be eating large quantities of the sea lettuce, indicating that other food items were in short supply at that time of year.

Sea lettuce thickets are home to literally hundreds of different kinds of vertebrate and invertebrate marine life, from young fishes to crustaceans and isopods. One common isopod is completely adapted to life on sea lettuce and as such is of an identical bright green color.

grudgingly recognizes the inherent value of those marginal lands now referred to, collectively and very much politically, as "wetlands." Whereas in the past, nary a thought was given to pressing the swamps into service as dumpsites or seedbeds for condo crops or strip mall agriculture, today the issue is debated, usually earnestly and with considerable forethought to the consequences—before the deed is eventually done anyway. For the unfortunate fact is that we are still losing wetlands in the United States today at the rate of about 100,000 acres a year. The destruction has been measurably slowed by a fresh tangle of legislation instituted by a growing host of defenders, but it takes a good deal of education and persuasion to counter the image of uselessness conjured up and long rooted in the public mind by the very word "swamp."

But in any event, Shark River's salt-

Black ducks. *This species, lacking in striking coloration though it is, is considered second only to the lordly canvasback as the "prince of waterfowl" among gunners. A strong, swift flier and extremely wary when under any hunting pressure, the black is a true bird of the coastal environment, preferring and associated with the vast expanses of salt marshes over freshwater habitats. Though closely related to the familiar mallard and identical to it in form, this duck can be told at once from the former by its uniformly dark dusky-brown color and by the white underwing linings, which flash conspicuously as the bird flies overhead.*

I have seen black ducks foraging unconcernedly on the estuary's beaches not thirty feet from bathers or people launching boats. This small group was on a marshy islet within a stone's throw of the sprawling Belmar Marina, one of the busiest anchorages in the state. I sketched them with a Berol Fineline pen, edging along the shore until I was about 20 feet from the dozing birds.

quick, rough sketch of gulls

Gulls panhandling for fish scraps. *This drawing illustrates the technique of creating rough, fast impressions of birds or animals moving too quickly or erratically to be captured by more deliberate, controlled methods. In this case, although there was a lot of confusing activity, the gulls, a mixed flock of laughing and ring-bills, were bucking a strong headwind, so that as they shifted back and forth and jockeyed for position just downwind of the fishing dock, they hung almost stationary on set wings rather than engaging in a lot of wild flapping action. This allowed for somewhat greater latitude in studying the birds' form and then capturing it in a few quick strokes on paper. For this rough sketch, I used a Berol Thinliner with a point slightly worn from past use; it gave me the slightly "dry brush" effect I was looking for.*

marsh habitat is not an extensive one—and, in fact, is not really a bona fide salt-marsh environment at all, but is rather of a brackish ecology. As compared with the vast sward of the real thing that still rims the broad bays that lie behind the barrier beaches in Ocean and Atlantic counties, the estuary's tidal marshes occupy no more than a couple of hundred acres of the back side of the bay's south arm and a few remnant enclaves in the Musquash Cove area—most of it simply fringe habitat less than 100 feet in width from the suburbanized woodlands to the low-tide waterline. True salt marshes occupy the low-lying areas behind barrier beaches on broad estuaries that have been partially sealed off from the sea by long-term siltation. Because Shark River's inlet is deep and broad and fast flowing and the boat traffic within the estuary quite heavy during the summer growing season, the littoral vegetation has little chance of effecting permanent colonization of the

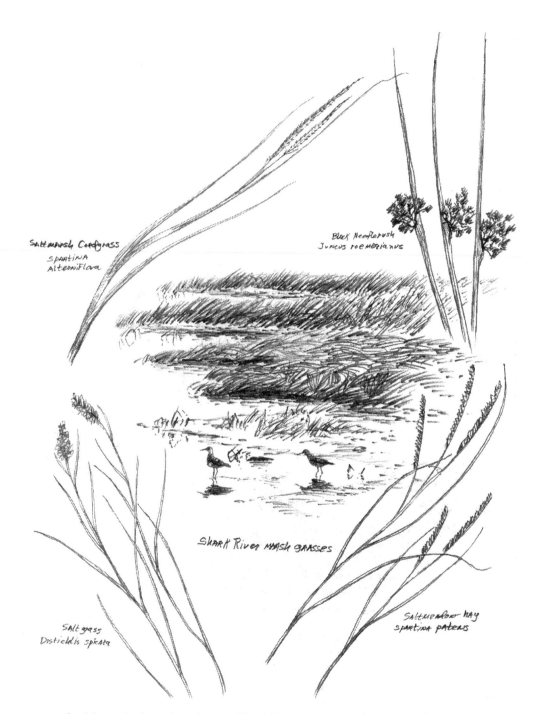

Saltmarsh Cordgrass
SPARTINA
AlterniFlora

Black NeedleRush
Juncus roemerianus

Salt grass
Disticklis spicata

Shark River marsh grasses

Saltmeadow hay
SPARTINA patens

Four species of tidal marsh plants found in the Shark River estuary. *Salt-marsh cordgrass (upper left) is the dominant marsh plant in the estuary's narrow fringe zone of wetlands that border the upper bay and river.*

Surprisingly green acres. *A quiet April afternoon on Musquash Cove offers reflections of semirural serenity counterpointed by the activity of a quartet of early-arriving summer laughing gulls. Although this vista has the look of the country to it, looks can be deceiving, for the well-populated borough of Neptune City lies just behind the scrim of trees on the north shore of the cove. Much, if not most, of the surviving woodland and marsh bordering the estuary has been set aside under the protection of current wetlands-protection laws or purchased by the state under its Green Acres program.*

Mute swans and double-crested cormorants in the shallow water of a nearby brackish pond. *A moment after I finished this drawing, the entire flock took flight and flew off across the pond. Swans taking wing from water are an incredible and very noisy sight; a veritable fusillade of spattering, splatting feet accompanied by loudly audible, swishing wingbeats make for quite a sight and sound show as the big, heavy, but famously graceful birds labor to become airborne.*

extensive mudflats. Not yet, at least, for the pattern of vegetation here is an ever-shifting one, with spartina and black rush beds gaining a foothold one year, only to vanish the next under the brief but savage assault of a powerful winter storm.

Although here and there along the muddy rim the shoreline is punctuated by the rotting hulks of abandoned boats—these lending an inadvertent aspect of the picturesque—the marshes are, as a whole, remarkably free of debris of the larger sort (bedsprings, pilfered shopping carts, old refrigerators, defunct car bodies, etc.). A significant percentage of the litter volume is composed of the plastic and

The estuary's south arm. *As I sat in the warming sun of April and drew this view, I was reminded of the words of New Jersey historian Gustav Kobbe, who observed in his 1889 book,* Jersey Coast and Pines, *that the shores of the Shark River estuary "are wooded and undulating. In the western horizon the hills rise to considerable height, and the general effect on a calm day is one of rare poetic beauty." Although this particular part of coastal New Jersey is today far from the somnolent rural enclave Kobbe knew in the previous century, the beauty and essential "rightness" of nature is still evident here if you seek it.*

aluminum "flotables" that enter the water via the pitching arms of summer boaters and which find their way here on the rising tide. But these are the ubiquitous artifacts of civilization that are virtually everywhere today.

But for me, the estuarine marshes mean the fish, in their crowds beyond counting and of at least thirty genera here. The fish of the brackish and marine littoral environment are by far the most abundant vertebrates: they are quite literally everywhere water is present, and their action and industry lend visible and fascinating interest to an otherwise underappreciated landscape.

Foremost among the estuary's "little fishes" is without a doubt the ubiquitous mummichog. Astonishingly common, it is the mainstay of the live bait industry everywhere it occurs and "forage" for just about every big fish that swims. But the 'chog is no biological dimwit, for in spite of its manifold natural enemies and humankind's relentless designs on its scaled hide, the fish persists in great numbers today, able to dodge disaster and survive conditions that would quickly kill most other fish. Indeed, it is the only fish able to survive as a permanent resident in the infamous Kill van Kull, that horrifyingly industrialized waterway that divides New York's Staten Island from New Jersey and has been called the most polluted little river in the world.

Outrageously common though it is, the adult mummichog—the breeding male, at least—is a most attractive little creature. In a sense, it suffers from the same "contempt of familiarity" that burdens the mallard duck ("it would be beautiful if it weren't so common"), but since the fish is virtually unknown to people other than anglers and ichthyologists, this is perhaps an unfair comparison. This little fish makes an excellent aquarium tenant, being agreeable by nature, easy to keep, and long-lived under halfway decent care.

Closely related to the mummichog but very different from it in coloration is the robust striped killifish, one of the largest of the North American killies. A "lunker" striped killy will stretch the tape at about seven inches and has actually been caught on hook and line, but the fish's most notable characteristics involve its color pattern and its behavior, both lending it a somewhat unique air among East Coast fishes. At Shark River, where this species occurs primarily over sandy bottoms, both sexes of this fish are correspondingly of a pale sandy brown color with silvery-white sides and belly. The male, however, is identified by his twelve dark crossbars, while his mate displays two to four black, broken horizontal stripes. This kind of permanent sexual dimorphism, or color difference

Tiger on the beach. *Stray house cats are not overly abundant around the estuary, and thus they don't figure as serious predators of native birds and small mammals, but a few, like this gray tom that hangs around one of the marinas, has become quite adept at hunting a rather unusual prey—the fiddler crab. Because fiddlers are just holding their own here, existing in a few scattered colonies, I've huffed stones at this guy (not, I must add, with intent to kill) whenever I've caught him stalking them. This time, I left him alone in the interest of artistic enterprise and watched him edge toward the crab burrows with the intensity of a leopard. A few crabs were up and about in the warm sun, but they apparently spotted him in time and he came up empty-pawed. From what I have observed in the past, he does eat those crabs he manages to bag.*

between the sexes, is rare among fishes in general, and unknown among the other species of killifishes occurring here.

The striped killy, and to some extent the mummichog, also has the uncanny ability to locate the water even if placed on a level beach some distance from the waterline; it will always flip-flop toward the life-sustaining water, even if it's well out of sight of the little jumper. This behavior is thought to have originated through the fish's habit of foraging in very shallow water during falling tides, at which times striped killies frequently find themselves stranded in rapidly

Boats and reed.

Dry-docked boats and reeds—two of the more characteristic features of the Shark River shoreline. *These craft, two pleasure boats (left) and a lobsterman (right), were transported to the storage area via a crane and a huge sling and then suspended while dock hands carefully stacked cement blocks beneath them as supports. This is one of the oldest, most reliable methods of supporting a boat rock-steady for the winter berthing season.*

emptying, landlocked mudflat pools.

One of the more engaging little salt-marsh fishes is the hyperactive and colorful sheepshead minnow. A true killifish, the sheepshead is a chunky little critter that looks more like a

sunfish and acts like one, too, for it is among the most pugnacious of fish in its size range—a mere three inches at maturity.

At most times of the year sheepsheads of both sexes are rather randomly mottled and silvery little creatures, their sole claims to fishy fame being their ceaseless activity and foul disposition. During the breeding season, however, the male's temper tantrums intensify, if that's possible, as does his raiment; he becomes a virtual gem of a fish, sporting a brilliant iridescent blue shoulder patch, salmon-pink sides and belly, and darkish fins edged with bright orange. A crowd of them wildly chasing the reluctant females around in a shallow marsh pool or narrow drainage ditch is a sight to behold—one of those unsung little spectaculars of nature to be found within sight and sound of New York or Atlantic City, and often outdoing those places in sheer glitter!

Sheepsheads occur from about Cape Cod south to the Rio Grande and are often fabulously abundant in extensive salt and brackish marshes. Shark River's total marsh area is definitely wanting, thus the fish is not a common sight here though the species does occur in some numbers in the quieter coves on the upper river, where the tidal infuence still makes itself felt.

Although the killifishes are usually the most active and apparent of the estuary's fishes and thus the most familiar to visitors, the roster by no means ends there. I invite the reader to peruse the Appendix at the end of this book for a more extensive, though certainly not exhaustive, list of species found in this square mile of New Jersey. A few of the more commonly encountered species will bear mentioning here.

Sticklebacks of two species (the two- and nine-spined varieties) prowl the shoreside weed beds from late March to late October. The two-spined stickleback is by far the commoner of the two, with as many as two dozen of the little fish being taken in a single seine haul over suitable habitat. Unlike the freshwater forms, the brackish two-spined species is not an overly colorful fish during the breeding season but is nonetheless an attractive creature in its own right. A mottled greenish gold, the tiny (two-inch) male becomes much brighter overall, and his pelvic fins turn a bright carmine red—about the only real color he'll ever have. Contrary to the popular image, these sticklebacks are not combative by nature but rather shy, retiring creatures that spend the bulk of their time furtively skulking in the dense eelgrass and wigeon grass thickets they call home.

Pipefishes and sea horses are present in the estuary nearly year-round, the former as always-abundant residents, the latter on a very much cyclic basis. Both animals are members of the family Sygnathidae, so that a pipefish, often incorrectly called "garfish" by the locals, is nothing more than a long, thin sea horse without a prehensile tail, and vice versa. Both animals absolutely depend on a healthy marine plant growth on the bay bottom for their tiny animal prey and for shelter and will decline if aquatic vegetation is damaged or destroyed by boats or dredging.

Sea horses may be absent from the estuary one year and virtually all over the place the next, this variation due to as yet unknown factors. One of my most exciting memories of life on the river involves the annual spring migration of sea horses into the estuary from the sea. The fish spend the winter months in warmer waters offshore, moving landward in May toward the benevolent weed beds of the estuary. I remember a dark, moonless night, the incoming tide running swift and silent past the docks of a marina, and in the pools of light shed upon the moving waters by the lights of the docks, hundreds and hundreds of little sea horses, twisting and turning, riding in with the flow. Animated little bits of flotsam, bravely passing through the bright lights of humans, coming in once again from the limitless sea in a timeless cycle, in just one of nature's myriad small wonders of animal journeys.

Shark River's inlet and estuary are also host in summer to piscine wayfarers from places much farther removed than offshore shoals. Butterflyfishes and angelfishes are normally thought of solely as exotic denizens of idyllic tropical reefs. For the most part, the reef environment is indeed the natural habitat of these colorful fishes as well as of a host of other tropical and subtropical species found with regularity here in the late summer and early fall.

The principal reason for this silent, intriguing yearly invasion of warmwater fishes is the Gulf Stream, that massive flow of tropical water that moves up the East Coast before veering out to sea north of Cape Cod. Many Floridian and Caribbean fishes begin to spawn in late March and April, and a great number of the newly hatched larval fishes, planktonic wanderers the size of a pinhead, are carried north on the Gulf Stream, dispersing coastwise as they grow, from Cape Cod to the Carolinas.

Most of these tropical transients find their way to sheltered bays and estuaries, where they put on size quickly in the warm, food-rich waters of the temperate summer. By August the butterflies and angels are recognizably such, in all their bright colors and trim forms, and their presence, especially in Shark River, attracts a sizable army of aquarist-divers who avidly collect the colorful creatures for aquaria. By mid-November, it's all over, for the great majority of these warmth-loving creatures perish before winter. Although there have been unconfirmed reports by divers of butterflyfishes prowling the jetty rocks in January, most of the little visitors grow lethargic in the chilling waters of early fall and are picked off by predators when the water temperature falls below fifty degrees. And thus this odd, rather pointless odyssey of fish migration comes to a rather ignominious end for yet another year.

As wonderful and varied as are the estuary's fishes, its invertebrate inhabitants are even more so, taking on the aspect of a "dust of stars" in sheer individual and specific numbers. Shark River's marshes and shallow waters are home to one major division of the world's invertebrates, the myriad crustacean genera. These run from the miniscule isopods and "beach hoppers" that fill every gallon of bay water with sparkling, swirling life to that formidably adaptable, pugnacious, and highly esteemed creature of the muddy bottoms and seafood platters, the blue crab.

The scientific name of the blue crab, *Callinectes sapidus*, is very fitting: the generic name means "beautiful swimmer," the specific, *sapidus*, is translated as "palatable or having an agreeable flavor." This amazing creature is today perhaps Shark River's preeminent littoral animal in both the biological and the gustatory perceptions of the phrase. With the

virtual disappearance of the oyster and the very real health perils attached to even contemplating dining on the estuary's bivalves, the blue, or blueclaw, crab is the only nonpiscine creature one may harvest for the table with reasonable safety. Although the Shark River estuary is not large enough to support much of a commercial crab fishery, several independent operators do maintain traplines in the south arm and a considerable host of locals and weekenders toss their collapsible wire traps from the many bridges and bulkheads in pursuit of the succulent, belligerent little beasties.

The blue crab is a commercially important animal throughout most of its sizable range—from southern New England south to the Gulf of Mexico and Yucatan—and it is subjected to intense pressure on both the commercial and recreational levels. Millions of pounds are harvested annually, and though the similarly exploited lobster stocks have undergone a slow but steady decline over the past twenty-five years due to overharvesting and habitat degradation, blue crab numbers appear to be holding their own in all but the most environmentally bankrupt areas. There certainly seems to be an adequate supply of them in Shark River.

The reason for the crab's persistent survivorship in a hostile world can be found in virtually every aspect of the creature's makeup—both physical and temperamental. It can be a real challenge to find a more aggressive, adaptable, efficiently designed aquatic predator than *Callinectes*. Any neophyte crabber who has attempted to remove a large and angry blueclaw from a trap with anything other than a whip and a chair knows that this animal will defend itself without hesitation, vigorously and often successfully against any adversary, regardless of size, and is well equipped to deliver a memorable pinch with its armored claws, or chelae.

Crabs will eagerly scavenge any and all dead animal matter, and at Shark River they are amazingly abundant around any marina docks where fish are cleaned and the racks and viscera thrown to the gulls. At night, when they are most active, prowling crabs can surprise and capture all but the fleetest of marine creatures, and little of living flesh is refused by a hungry blueclaw. Although it was long believed that the blue crab will refuse to eat another of its own kind (crabbers still avoid baiting a trap with dead crabs), recent studies indicate that they are strongly cannibalistic. Research involving the gut contents of 1,600 Chesapeake Bay blueclaws revealed that nearly 40 percent of the contents consisted of crab parts, with the larger crabs eating smaller crabs and more

crabmeat. In Shark River, the favored food—after fish-cleaning refuse—of the blue crab appears to be soft-shell clams, the relatively fragile nature of the shell making it easy for a big crab to crush and extract the meat.

Taxonomically, *Callinectes* is a member of the "swimming crab" group, which includes the slightly smaller, though no less foul-tempered, calico crab, or lady crab, popular as striped bass bait. The rear pair of legs is modified into flattened, paddlelike appendages that offer the crab a high degree of maneuverability anywhere in the water column, from the bottom to the surface, where individuals are often seen sculling energetically about at night.

In addition to its formidable hunting abilities and superb adaptability, *Callinectes* is really a most attractive creature. Although its carapace (the back shell) is a rather somber darkish olive-green, its underside and legs, including the dangerous claws, are a clear white beautifully accented by touches of bright vermillion and an almost psychedelic blue. In the hand or in the trap, there's no mistaking a blue crab, for no other local crustacean even approaches it in colorful raiment.

Blue crabs, like all crustaceans, undergo periodic moltings of the outer shell, or exoskeleton, during the natural life span. In its normal state it is called a

Fish neighbors. *All these fishes are found in abundance in the Shark River estuary and among the rocks at the inlet's mouth. The most appealing creature, the sea horse, fluctuates widely in occurrence from year to year, being quite common one summer and virtually absent the next. Clockwise from top right: the tautog, or blackfish; the American eel; the northern pipefish; the sheepshead minnow, the mummichog; a pair of striped killies, the male below; the conner, or bergall, the northern, or lined, sea horse; and the three-spined stickleback.*

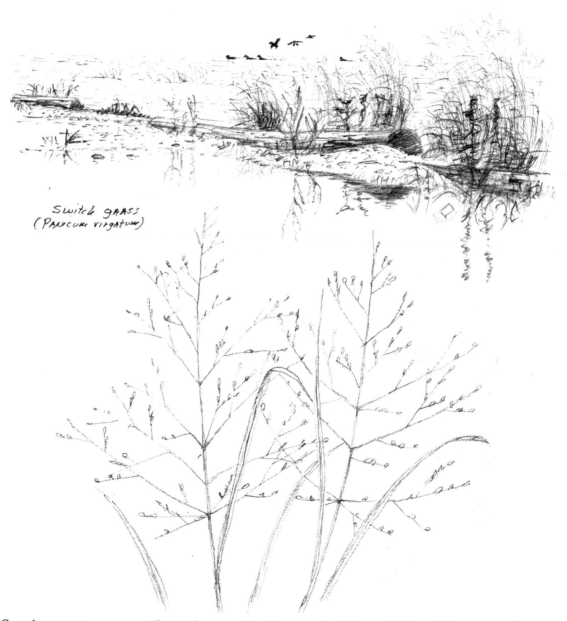

Switch grass
(Panicum virgatum)

Switch, or panic grass—a tall, stately perennial. *Because of its ability to colonize and thrive in severely disturbed and altered habitats, this grass is universally regarded as a mere "weed." The plant is not partial to the seaside environment, but rather is found in many situations far inland, for the most part in places like old landfills, roadsides, and other damaged habitats. These windblown stands of the plant are growing behind the old telephone poles that mark the boundary of a parking lot right at the bay's edge. The plants are regularly submerged by higher tides, giving testament to this grass's ability to survive immersion in salt water.*

"hard-shell crab." Immediately prior to shedding its old skin, the crab senses its growing vulnerability and seeks a sheltered hiding place in which it can complete the process in relative safety. At this point, the crab is known as a shedder, or peeler. When the molt is completed, a process that may take an hour or two, the crab is in its highest state of vulnerability until its new exoskeleton hardens, usually within a two- to four-hour period. At this time the animal moves about as little as it can manage and can be picked up by hand with minimal risk of a pinch; these are the much more expensive "soft-shell crabs" of the fish markets.

Virtually nothing even remotely edible escapes the attention of a hungry blue crab, and this King Kong-sized appetite, along with the crab's determination to satisfy it at all costs, has placed *Callinectes sapidus* squarely into a predator-prey relationship with the most efficient predators of all—humans.

There are no meaningful recent figures available on the Shark River blue-crab fishery because so many of them, in fact the majority, are taken by recreational crabbers who are not required to report anything to "the proper authorities." All along the 127-mile length of the Jersey shore in summer, though, many thousands of pounds of the succulent crustaceans are harvested. From the turbid waters of Raritan Bay (where warnings against seafood consumption are issued with depressing regularity) to the broad shallows of Delaware Bay to the south, the blue crab is king to the guy with a few bucks for the gas to get there and a ripe chicken neck and a wire trap to do the catching.

There is, of course, more than one way to catch a crab. Given the creature's constant rovings and unerring ability to locate and follow the scent of carrion in the water to its source, the would-be crabber has only to provide that source, surround it with any one of several clever contrivances designed to outwit crabs, and hope for the best.

The one method requiring the least amount of effort on the part of the crabber, and thus the most popular, is the wire crab trap. Coming in a number of designs, with two types—the folding trap and the maze—in the most common usage, a trap has only to be baited with the most aromatic attractant available and left for the quarry to locate and enter. The folding trap, of either square or pyramidal construction, is simply dropped to the bottom and then quickly lifted and checked every five minutes or so, depending on how abundant crabs have proven to be in a given locality. The contraption flops into an open position when it hits the substrate, with the bait, usually a chicken neck or fish head, in the center. Fishes will regard such an alien object suddenly appearing in their environment with considerable suspicion, but a blue crab, wily as it is in all other respects, simply fails to recognize the metal gridwork of a trap as a potential danger and strolls right over it for the meal it sees there. But this is where its naïveté ends, for as quickly as a lifted crab trap snaps shut, many would-be captives evade its clutches; few marine creatures can move faster than a blue crab that senses that something has evil designs on its armored hide. Based on my own underwater observations of a crab trap in action in good crab turf, many adult crabs do escape, and rather easily, going swiftly up and over the wire the second the cage begins to close. They are amazingly facile critters, crabs!

The maze-type trap, homemade and used principally by commercial crabbers, is a rather weighty, ponderous object, but it is much more lethal to crabs and therefore its use is licensed. In essence, this trap is a large cage constructed of tar or rubber-coated chicken wire and measuring about four feet square. Although the design may vary according to the builder, this trap operates on the "easy to get into but hard to get out of" principle employed in minnow traps. Entry into the inner, baited chamber is gained through a narrow slot at the end of a rectangular funnel placed in the trap's side. The bait, normally a whole menhaden, or "bunker" in New Jersey parlance, is contained within a small wire mesh canister in the trap's inner chamber.

These traps are secured to a series of stakes driven into the bottom mud; in Shark River the traplines are usually situated in the shallow areas of the south arm of the estuary, where they can be checked on foot every twelve hours at low tides. In good years, the commercial crabbers can harvest tons of crabs with smaller commercial crabbers and just perhaps stay ahead of the tax collector and break even.

Traps and other mechanical gear are mainly the province of the serious recreational or commercial crabbers; for the weekend "crab dipper," by far the commonest human predator on crabs found on the estuary, all that's required are an inexpensive dip net, a chicken neck, a length of string, and no small amount of fast reflexes. In dipping, or "baiting," the bait is lowered to the bottom via the twine and left there until a crab with an appetite locates it. The animal will usually grasp the chicken neck and hunker down on the spot for a meal, so it's imperative that the crabber keep a taut line, so as to feel the lightest touch of the quarry. The bait is then drawn easily and slowly upward—with the distracted diner attached—until the

Some characteristic plants of the harsh, seaside environment.

ready net can be slipped under it. It sounds like a ridiculously easy operation and it is—usually. In most cases the crab is so preoccupied with the food at hand (or claw, as the case may be) that it's no great challenge to draw it near enough to slip the net underneath it. But not always, for the blueclaw reacts instantly to sudden movement and can release the bait and simply drop from sight with truly amazing speed. As might be guessed, crab baiting is best carried out by two people: one to handle the bait and the other keeping the net at the ready as the potential "shore dinner" hovers into view.

But if you must handle a big blue, care, of course, is the watchword. Crabs possess more than adequate eyesight, even when stranded on land, and will swiftly turn and face an enemy, clapping their formidable chelae together whenever a part of the enemy's anatomy comes within range. Like a snapping turtle, the blue crab knows the difference between a stick and a finger—it will quickly release the former but hang on like death to the latter if it connects with it. A large blue crab can put some real power behind a pinch—enough to draw blood in an adult and lacerate the finger of a careless youngster. About the safest way to pick up a live blueclaw is to pin it with a net or a balled-up towel and grab it from behind with thumb and forefinger. The animal is quite dexterous, but it cannot reach back over its own shell or very far beneath itself if held facing away from you. In any case, a lively, full-of-fight crab should not be fondled or examined at length but dropped with dispatch into the waiting bucket. When it comes to sketching the animals, my method for the drawings that appear here was to place the live crabs in the freezer for about fifteen minutes. This rendered them sluggish and lethargic to the point of handleability but posed no threat to their survival; they were released (honest!) following the posing session.

The ultimate purpose of recreational crabbing is in the eating, and the successful crabber has only to maneuver the reluctant catch into the proverbial watched pot and boil away for the taste treat of nonpareil seafood.

Whatever the fate of the individual blue crab at the hand of a human, of far greater concern is that of the future of the species itself in an increasingly perilous environment. For the moment, the blueclaws of Shark River, as well as those elsewhere along the Jersey shore, seem in no immediate danger of extirpation. The Raritan–New York bay complex contains some of the most degraded and toxic aquatic habitats on earth, yet it literally crawls with blue crabs. Although the sale and consumption of crabs taken from the complex is prohibited, the residents of the metro region often disregard the warnings of officialdom and dine on them with gusto, some hardy souls steaming their catches in little pots set on Coleman stoves on the docks of the lower Hudson and at Bayonne. Here,

eel fykes at low tide

Eel fykes at low tide. *The south arm of the estuary is a broad, shallow body of water heavily utilized by both commercial eel fishermen and crab-pot operators. The fyke traps and pot spreads are often so numerous in "good years" that they present some hazard to navigation for recreational boaters and waterskiers, and the issue has generated numerous complaints by the latter. The dispute is a near-classic example of the increasingly abrasive confrontation between those who utilize a habitat as a source of livelihood and those who play in it, in the process pumping recreational dollars into the local economy. Summer visitors have also been known to tamper with eel and crabbing gear, helping themselves to the catch, with the predictable, and sometimes violent, reaction from the beleaguered fishermen.*

the crabbers pursue their sport with a mixture of fatalism, defiance, and an odd sense of immediacy that bespeaks the "live for today" philosophy.

The "beautiful swimmer" is Shark River's consummate crustacean inhabitant. The artfully freckled lady, or calico, crab is tops in the minds of striped bass fishermen, for it makes the best bait for that great game fish; beachcombers and waders of the summer shallows find endless fascination in the feisty, ever-restless little hermit crabs; green crabs scuttle about their dock-piling high rises; and the ponderous rock and Jonah crabs prowl the kelp-girt rocks of the jetties. But *Callinectes* alone enjoys such an exalted, cosmopolitan presence in the estuary; it is the perennial survivor among the brute creation here, found in the murkiest waters and known and pursued by all with a yen for prime seafare.

Black-crowned night herons
7/29/91

Popular perches. *Manmade objects in the otherwise broad, flat estuarine environment are always popular with coastal birds as perches—and for a variety of reasons. Most water birds employ them as vantage points in the eternal search for food or as resting stations at which to attend to their toilet. Though a small and temporary territory, a dock piling or a marker buoy is a territory nonetheless and vigorously defended against would-be interlopers, unless they be larger and more dominant individuals of the same species.*

The engaging little scenario (upper sketch), which occupied the better part of an hour, took place on a channel buoy and was obviously an avian romance in full bloom. The male tern performed repeated aerial gymnastics to impress his lady love, bringing at least ten fish offerings to her in the process.

The dock pilings of the main inlet channel are often occupied by larger avian fishermen, such as these black-crowned night herons. I sketched this trio shortly after dawn, as they were "winding down" after a night's angling activity. They were vaguely apprehensive of my near presence, but aside from some nervous neck stretching and foot shifting, they remained doggedly where they were. The incidence of this night heron has increased somewhat in the Shark River estuary over the past few years; scattered pairs nest in the taller trees of the fairly extensive wooded area at the head of the bay.

Part IV

Nightfall; the Upper River; Turtles

Upper Shark River. *Where the sea's tides meet and meld with the freshwater flow of the uplands, the scene is still one of relatively unspoiled nature in spite of the fact that residential development surrounds the river and estuary— just out of sight. This is due primarily to the buffer of protected wetlands and riverine forest that line the river here, a relatively rare act of ecological foresight on the part of officialdom when dealing with the living environment.*

It was not always that way, however. If a grandiose nineteenth-century engineering scheme designed to transform Shark River into a cross-state shipping canal had come to fruition, who knows what manner of watercourse would exist here today?

Today, the upper Shark River drains a large area of agricultural and suburban infrastructure as well as scattered enclaves of undeveloped land. As such, the waterway receives a considerable amount of organic nutrients via surface runoff and delivers them to the estuary. In spite of its inevitably degraded state, Shark River remains an important place of recreation and is heavily utilized by both boaters and anglers during the summer months. It remains a place of special beauty and vitality, a haven of solitude in the midst of the confusion and cacophony of the modern-day Jersey shore.

The sight, sound, and scent of the earth's living waters have since time immemorial had a deep and profound appeal to the great majority of humanity. The vast ocean and the multitudes of rivers great and small that serve it seem to occupy a primeval, spiritual place in the collective consciousness. So much so that, wherever there is a shoreline, there will be found people, drawn there by an undefinable need and in greater numbers today than will be found anywhere else. Whether to simply drive to a dead-end road at the edge of the sea on a summer day and stand and gaze upon the mysterious and primal deep for a few minutes, or to dream of a happy home by the riverside, the presence of water speaks to the human heart in a timeless and very intimate way.

Monmouth County's abundant humanity gathers at the river that empties into the Shark River estuary with something of a patchwork-quilt contradiction of distance and familiarity. There is no doubt that much, if not most, of the Shark River watershed is suburban in nature. But although the region as a whole is well populated with corporate "parks" and upscale housing developments, much of the immediate environs of the waterway has been afforded protection from development—for now, at least—in some form of seminatural or recreational form. Much of the river's shoreline within five miles of the estuary consists of brackish marsh and thus comes under the tenuous protection of New Jersey's wetlands protection legislation. Add to this the fact that much of the truly "upper river," some thirty miles distant from the inlet's mouth, lies within the sprawling, and mostly wooded, military facilities of ECOM-EVANS and the Earle Naval Weapons Depot, and you have the principal reason why this river has, for the most part, escaped the severe degradation common to aquatic habitats in the urban Northeast.

For much of Shark River's upper reaches, that part of the river that lies well beyond the square mile of the estuary, the waterway is relatively clear and only mildly burdened with construction and road runoff, and moves through fairly extensive tracts of undisturbed forest. Closer to the coast, Shark River gathers volume from several small feeder tributaries; the current slows, the stream acquires some

The East End Avenue, or Tucker's Point, bridge. *Recently rebuilt, this bridge hosts a dedicated crowd of fair-weather crabbers and snapper fishermen who line the rails from bank to bank when the sun's hot, the tide's right, and the fish are running.*

depth, and then meets the vanguard of the tide; here, it meanders placidly through the sylvan banks that define the environs of the sprawling Shark River Park and Golf Course complex. It thence enters the true estuarine world, the lush, grassy sward of the brackish marshes at the head of the bay.

It is at the point of this subtle, indeed invisible, confluence of sea- and sweetwater, within sight of the harbor and its square mile of rich, shallow littoral, that the worlds of people and nature coexisting in uneasy communion come together and attain perhaps their most appealing blend of physical coexistence. That this is so can be seen at once when one takes in the view from the bridge.

The Brighton Avenue bridge crosses

the Shark River at a point just out of sight of the estuary itself. Here, the river is fairly broad, very much tidal in character, and flanked by an attendant sward of salt marshes; altogether, the scene has a distinctly pastoral look to it, most especially in the soft light of an early summer day. To the northwest, the stream rounds a bucolic, sedgy bend and passes beneath the Route 18 bridge. The structure interrupts, but does not destroy, the image of verdant peace; it's simply there—low-slung, utilitarian, unadorned by frivolous architectural embellishments, the soft, day-and-night rush of traffic giving away its purpose. In the view to the southeast, the little valley effects a sharp curve due east toward the sea; the marshes here are bounded by the low, wooded flanks of the Shark River Hills, these dense with greenery that effectively conceals the

'26/91

Natural features—and eyesores. *This tranquil little cove, on the east shore of the estuary, is the very picture of the "scenic shoreside" when the tide is high. At mean low tide, civilization's discards in varying stages of disintegration are revealed, including rusting stanchions, waterlogged boards, and an old tire. Most of these items were likely chucked from the dock in the foreground, the remains of which slowly yield to the endless and patient cycle of the passing years and the workings of the elements. The littoral environment, perhaps more than any other, illustrates the transient nature of human artifacts; in time, the sea reclaims all, whether it be trash or treasure.*

The Brighton Avenue bridge, winter scene, marsh and river partially frozen. 1/3/92

The Brighton Avenue bridge. *This bridge is not a structure designed to regale the eye with soaring, Verrazanolike grace of form, but it performs its assigned task, that of delivering the cars of the resident suburbanites across the upper Shark River in dry-tired safety, with utilitarian adequacy. And all with no complaint save the occasional creak and groan of heavy, creosoted support timbers.*

**A resident cardinal surveying the beach from the vantage of a bulkhead post sporting a "no clamming"
sign.** *The state Department of Environmental Protection has closed the entire estuary to the harvest of bivalves for
human consumption, and these characteristic red warning signs are to be seen everywhere along the shoreline,
especially in those locations permitting public access to the mudflats. The warnings are a sad commentary on the
general state of affairs of estuaries everywhere in the Northeast.*

scores of modest homes that have been
built here over many years. The bay,
broad and flat and china blue, lies
furrowed under sail and motor; the
seaside towns beyond, on the eastern
shore, rim the entire north-south span
of the horizon, a rippled mirage,
dreaming in the summer haze. The sky
is never empty of birds.

After nightfall, however, the bridge
environs undergo something of a
transformation. The bright lights of
Belmar and of the eastern terminus
of I-195 in Wall Township to the
southeast are hidden by the thickly
wooded and still uninhabited point of
land that extends into the bay at the
river's mouth, and on windless nights,
banks and soft rills of light, airy fog
move in a silent flood up the watercourse

and fill the valley with ghosts. At night, this section of the Shark River can be a dark and vaguely forbidding place, surrounded though it is by the crowded familiarity of suburban New Jersey.

In an age accustomed to the soaring, impersonal utility of turnpike and freeway bridges, the Brighton Avenue bridge presents an almost quaint, countrified contrast. It is a rather narrow two-laner of heavy, rumble-prone planking surfaced with asphalt and timber construction, lying about 300 yards east of Marconi Road, named for the Italian electrical engineer and inventor of the wireless, Guglielmo Marconi.

Vehicular traffic over the Brighton Avenue bridge can be fairly heavy during the day, and during the long summer months its railings are a popular fishing and loafing spot. But late at night, the isolated intersection and the crossing beyond it take on an aspect of the past century. In spite of the close proximity of the heavily traveled state Route 18 and the presence of three tepid streetlamps at this crossing of road and river, an odd sense of otherworldliness often makes itself felt here in the midnight hours. The black, slowly moving river burbles fitfully beneath the span, and the surrounding, silent woods only reluctantly admit the scattered, winking lights of the very contemporary homes

A rugged but effective wooden bulkhead. *This is typical of the many bulkheads fending off the effects of wind and wave all over the estuary.*

The Marconi Transoceanic wireless compound — a bit overgrown by time and... 1/7/92

A derelict sewage-treatment plant. *On the wooded bluff overlooking the estuary.*

one knows are just around the corner and up the hill. It is as though one might, topping the gentle rise and descending toward the bridge, come upon some mournful, wandering phantom, the ghost of a long-dead colonial farmer, or perhaps the mournful shape of Marconi himself, leaning into the sea wind at the span's rough-hewn rail and unhappily surveying the neglected memorial to his earthly accomplishments. Or worse, the nocturnal traveler just might encounter some great, armored, prehistoric-looking beastie laboriously hauling itself dripping from the dark tides of the river and invading the sanctity of the

quiet and familiar suburban road . . . just as I did one dark June night.

If you look toward the sea on this part of the northern New Jersey coast, you can't see the stars, even on a clear night; the illuminations of the oceanic strip of resort towns are just too bright and overwhelm the cosmic light show of the heavens. To the west, the wonderful deeps of the night sky still hold sway—the illuminatory din of Philadelphia and Camden are mercifully distant—and a scattering of stars grace the dome of heaven. Not the dusts of infinity one might look upon and try to comprehend deep in the mountains of a roadless area, mind you, but a rare enough privilege in the Northeast, where an urban child may never—really never—witness firsthand the splendor of the Milky Way.

As I topped the rise in the road that descends in a gentle curve to the Brighton Avenue bridge, I gawked up through my van's windshield at the universe that presented itself to all who ventured to retreat from the "dross of life" for but a minute and take in the view. We know that the earth is but a mote of planetary dust suspended in the void and of next to no significance by the standards of the infinite cosmos, yet one tends to take the earthcentric view nonetheless. The earth is home to humanity, and the living of the life it provides is quite filled with the drossness of daily survival.

It had begun to rain, soft, warm, and pleasing on this deep-shadowed June

Tidbits of human history near the shore. *This completely unobstrusive "monument" marks the site of Guglielmo Marconi's first trans-Atlantic transmission by wireless.*

snapping turtle
(Chelydra serpentina)

Snapping turtle. *When does a "big" snapper become a "monster" snapper? When it passes the thirty-pound mark. The common snapping turtle (*Chelydra serpentina*) is the third-largest North American reptile, exceeded only by the American alligator (the crocodilian) and the alligator snapper of the southern states. Forty- to fifty-pound common snappers have been reported, but most average in the fifteen- to twenty-pound range—a formidable creature nonetheless.*

This rough drawing was done from a "pet" animal owned by a friend; it weighs about sixteen pounds and, as might be suggested in the detail of the formidably armored head, it is not a creature begging to be petted or otherwise "related" to! Snappers are sometimes seen laboriously crossing the back roads of the upper river area during the late spring and early summer.

Shark River's main branch, rising from forested wetlands about fifteen miles west of the estuary. *Although there are scattered homes in the immediate area, the watershed is quite rural and relatively undisturbed (for New Jersey).*

I sketched the picturesque watercourse from a small bridge under which moved the shallow, clear, entirely fresh waters of the upper river. The late afternoon was quiet, chill, and overcast, the surrounding woodlands bereft of birdsong. Occasional shotgun reports reverberated off the low hills nearby, however. The surrounding woods were fairly recently cutover and thus a massed tangle of small trees and dense thickets of Virgina creeper and barberry— very difficult to suggest in line. I attempted this through the use of vertical strokes accented by quick horizontal line work to indicate the ranks of saplings that constituted most of the growth in the background.

The floating dock. *This structure is the logical response to the problem of siting a stable, accessible anchorage on water that rises and falls by several feet twice a day. The floater eliminates the need to clamber down an algae-slimed ladder to one's boat at low tide; whether the tide is high or low, this dock is always right where it's needed—at the same level as the waiting boat. Most smaller floating docks, such as this one situated in a marshy cove, are secured to two or more stout uprights by a U-clamp, which allows the dock upward and downward—but not lateral—movement as the tide rises or falls.*

night. I pulled my gaze away from the sky . . . and saw the turtle square in the middle of the road. It was just beyond the bridge, a great black heap in the center of the roadway, the size of a washtub. I hauled on the wheel; the van swerved, slipped, and slewed, and passed over it.

The locals talked of huge snappers in the river, even in the strongly saline tidal portions, but I had never seen one, not even a pathetic roadkill, crushed and violated by the endless, impersonal traffic. It has been estimated that a coastal creek two miles long may harbor a dozen or more large adult snappers and at least a hundred smaller juveniles. That this may be so in the Shark River can be seen in the rapid decimation of mallard broods on the upper river; it is rare to see a watchful hen with more than four or five

Migrating tree swallows. *This gathering of birds is one of the exciting little events of nature that afford one a small insight into the vast workings of the cosmic biological clock. At Shark River these swallows congregate along the north shore of the southern arm of the estuary, attracted not only by the abundant flying insects there but by a large stand of bayberry bushes laden with ripening fruit in midsummer.*

On the day I sketched this gathering flock, many individuals passed within a few feet of me and perched unconcernedly on nearby pilings. The tree swallow is not normally thought of as a "beach bird," but it is very common and highly conspicuous at Shark River throughout the warmer months.

ducklings when the normal clutch of eggs may number between twelve and sixteen. In any case, the snapping turtle is the only turtle species likely to be encountered in the estuarine environment, with the possible exception of the now scarce diamondback terrapin. Snappers are important predators on the young of waterfowl wherever the big reptiles occur in any abundance at all. I had seen big snappers engaged in their slow-motion yet ferocious territorial battles or more restrained mating rituals on the open water, these accompanied by much plunging and rolling and splashing about, but had never spotted one attempting an overland journey here. The sight of the monster in the middle of the road was a jarring surprise, to say the least.

I slowly backed up, stopped, and put on my emergency flashers. Close up, the animal was truly impressive. A prehistoric visitor indeed, its rain-wet, heavily armored shell and mailed head looked absolutely impervious to any and all threats a world of mere mortals could hurl against it. It must have weighed forty pounds and was likely a female on her annual search for a land-based depository for her future generations. She lay there, lumplike and secure, in the middle of the wet-glistening roadway, regarded me with an eye as steely and emotionless as a ball bearing, and slowly opened her ridged, hook-billed jaws. And waited, unassailable, impregnable.

But of course, she was far from that. The next passing car or truck, due along surely within minutes and perhaps driven by one less motivated by conscience than I, would do her in with

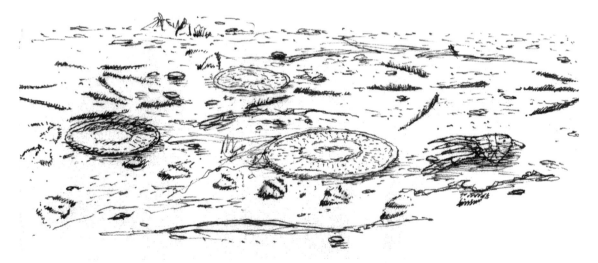

Gelatinous remains of stranded moon jellyfish. *One of the more common sights along the summer beaches, these remains look something like transparent, rubbery flapjacks. An abundance of these hapless creatures on a bathing beach never fails to elicit disgust among human beachgoers, who may venture to poke the dead animals with sticks rather than touch them, out of needless fear—in this species—of "jellyfish stings." Jellyfish are composed almost entirely of water and soon desiccate and shrivel away under the hot summer sun.*

These "jellies" came ashore on the low-tide mudflat the day after a moderate coastal storm; although the surrounding mud was intricately scribed by a network of duck, gull, and egret tracks, the birds obviously saw nothing of gustatory value in them for the flattened bodies were undamaged.

violent ease. Not even the largest turtle can survive a confrontation with motorized man. It is something of an irony that a human perhaps unaccustomed to effort beyond that of changing channels on a television set could, with the lightest of pressure of foot on an accelerator pedal, physically demolish a creature that had evolved over the countless eons to withstand all manner of natural perils.

I gazed at the huge beast hunched motionlessly on the road before me and

sighed; she would have to be moved to safety.

The snapping turtle is one of those creatures burdened with the apparent need to justify its existence to humankind, the steward of the planet. It is a large, rather dim-witted, physically unattractive (to human eyes) animal that has never learned to adapt to other creatures that share its world, except to serve as prey. The snapper knows no fear because there is nothing within its timeless, inherited experience and

Derelict structures. *Change is in fact an enduring fact of life on the estuary, as will be seen in the considerable number of derelict structures lining the shoreline, some simply unattractive, others so weathered and worn that they appear as little more than oddly fitting constructions, extensions of the natural scene. Docks and wharves are the logical, and thus the most common, constructions along any developed shoreline, and the Shark River estuary's perimeters are ringed with dozens of them in varying stages of usefulness. The old pier is a rather recent victim of wind and tide—about five years ago it met its end in a powerful coastal storm.*

Butterfly season. *August and September are the months of the monarch butterflies at Shark River. It's quite surprising to see these large black-and-orange butterflies lazily but somehow "intently" winging their way across the open waters of the estuary or even arriving at the ocean beaches seemingly from across the sea! Many of the butterflies observed here flying southwestward in August and September are spotted following the bulkhead along the north shore of the south cove, where the prevailing southwest winds provide both lift and impetus to the flights.*

The monarch is one of the relatively few insects that undertakes extended, seasonal migrations in the manner of birds. Virtually all of North America's monarch butterfly population converges on several, extremely localized (and thus vulnerable) wintering "roosts" in southern California and Mexico.

oh-so-slowly evolving psyche that it need fear. Raccoons and skunks may locate the nests and eat the eggs or hatchlings, but they wouldn't dream of trifling with an adult turtle; a big adult snapper fears nothing and no one, not even a human, for the animal is absolutely incapable of that emotion. People are the only creatures alive today equipped to destroy a large snapper with impunity, but the reptile cannot, of course, recognize that fact. The land-stranded snapper sees an approaching human simply as an object differing little in form and threat from a cow, an equally massive presense incapable of violence against it. The average snapper may be a virtual zoo of parasites: leeches festoon its scaly hide, while heartworms, nematodes, and other creepie crawlies inhabit its innards. But in spite of these considerable organic burdens, a snapping turtle that manages to escape being run over by a car or captured for the limited "turtle soup" market may live

great blue heron in pine
10/10/91

Great blue heron. *Although these birds do it all the time and in fact nest in high-timber rookeries, it's still something of an oddity to see such a large, awkward-looking heron perched high in a tree. Watching one plane sedately into the tangle of a treetop, settle uncertainly like a long-legged kite, and attempt to rearrange its spindly legs and toes and grope for a foothold in the maze of upper branches can be one of nature's more hilarious sights!*

Domestic geese foraging at Memorial Park, Shark River. *These impressive birds, which may weigh up to 30 pounds, are determined grazers and have been the source of some complaints by park visitors owing to the treacherous walking conditions created by their very ample droppings.*

I offered these birds a few slices of wheat bread to "bait" them to my spot and then drew them as they slowly lost interest in me and moved off, grazing as they went. The sketches were done with a combination of HB hard and soft carbon pencils.

for up to sixty years, a respectable age in any book.

The snapper sees no reason to fawn, grovel, to apologize for nothing and to no one, and has one of the foulest tempers in all of animaldom—it's an animal with a very bad reputation indeed.

Snapping turtles are indeed dangerous creatures and even in the smaller sizes can inflict considerable damage to the extremities of the unwary. Its bite is swift, generally unerring, and tenacious, although there is no truth to the old saw that a snapper will release its grip and wander off at sundown. But as with most animals that are not friendly toward humans, a vast gulf separates myth and reality when it comes to *Chelydra serpentina*'s threat to life or limb. For one thing, even the largest snapper cannot break a broomstick with its bite—a common yarn even among experienced outdoorspeople who would know better if they had put the tale to the test. The snapper's bite is loaded with power and strength, but there is a vast difference

geese : goslings
Shark River, July 4 '91

Goose families. *In late June Shark River Park's resident domestic geese appear, escorting broods of downy young on the upper river and venturing down the estuary as far as the salt-marsh zone. At this time, the normally placid geese become much more wary of human approach and can be quite aggressive (and potentially dangerous) toward small children that innocently approach the appealing goslings too closely. Being large and formidable, these geese manage to bring the majority of their young to maturity without incident, though they do lose some to the depredations of snapping turtles and, when the goslings are smaller, to prowling raccoons. I drew this pair and family with a Micro Permaroller fine-point pen.*

Young poplars and red maples. *Trees bisect the grassy sward of the riverbank with late-afternoon sun-shadows. This seemingly natural scene is in reality the crest of an old landfill site, the trees having taken root from arriving seeds and, perched right of that, the bluff of the little hill, having escaped the mowers of town crews cutting the remainder of the small state-owned Green Acres "parklet."*

between a wooden broomstick and a flesh-and-blood finger, which a very large turtle can sever with ease.

Many people will refrain from swimming in a lake when informed that snappers inhabit it, but the snapping turtle is truly dangerous—and then just to the foolhardy—only when it is encountered out of its element—the water—and thus at a distinct

"This old house." Last year's home of a pair of mockingbirds disinteg in spring winds and rains. 4/1/00

The tattered, unraveling remains of an old mockingbird's nest clinging conspicuously and precariously to a dogwood branch. *The nest was a curious collection of materials of both the natural and the artificial; assorted grasses and twigs were intertwined with a tangle of brightly colored yarn, bits of aluminum foil, and long strips of plastic, a testimony to the birds' resourcefulness and adaptation to the home-building materials at hand.*

disadvantage. Submerged, a snapper is an introverted pussycat; it diligently avoids contact with humans or other animals too large to be considered prey and seldom, if ever, strikes while underwater, even in defense. I've encountered large snappers during the course of lake and bog dives and have poked them (with sticks, of course!) to the point of exasperation for both of us, with the only reaction being the patient desire to escape the human pest. Most snapping turtles observed (and left in peace) in the wild present anything but a savage mien. The usual "sighting" involves the merest glimpse of a dark snout and beady eyes poking above the water's surface and taking a furtive look around; approach on foot or by boat and the turtle ducks below with scarcely a ripple and vacates the premises as quickly as it can manage.

On land it's a different matter. Here the turtle is vulnerable, knows it, and acts accordingly if threatened. The snapper is a strictly aquatic animal that is found ashore on only two occasions during its life: when the hatchling female emerges from the egg, struggles to ground level, and makes that perilous trek to the safety of the water, and when she must come ashore again to lay her eggs in the nurturing earth. The male makes only the first foray, for adult snappers in an amorous frame of mind encounter each other and mate entirely within the dim havens of their waterworld.

The female snapper may journey up to a mile from the home lake or river in search of a nest site, no mean feat for an animal so heavy and thus ungainly on land. But if surprised, she does not timidly withdraw into the safety of her shell as do most other, more mildly disposed species of turtles, for in addition to the act of fleeing being an alien one, she physically cannot. The snapper's shell and plastron, meager in construction and incapable of offering their owner secure refuge, have been designed by nature for a fearless, heavily armored creature with few natural enemies and unaccustomed to retreat; the plastron is a mere shield, protecting the vulnerable underside and the entrails within. Thus the threatened snapper never cringes but rather affects an odd, stiff-legged, open-mouthed defense posture and waits for the enemy to make the next move.

I moved closer to the big turtle and, glancing up and down the still-empty roadway, squatted in front of her dark, motionless form. She turned her mailed head slightly, pale pinkish mouth agape, and eyed me impassively. I wondered how old she was; from the looks of her and from her great size, I surmised she must have survived many seasons—perhaps twenty-five—on the estuary, many such perilous land journeys,

encountering a great host of other creatures in her travels and surviving countless attempts on her life in the dark waters of this tidal river.

I waved my hand in front of her, at what I hoped was a safe distance; the turtle hissed faintly and only widened her pale, ominous gape a little. I was inexplicably prodded by some interior imp to tempt fate and flipped and wiggled my hand a little closer to the ugly, tubular snout. In an instant, the creature vented a quick, sharp hiss and struck; my reactions were good, and her jaws came together with a hollow "clop!" It was without a doubt one of the more sinister and menacing sounds I had ever heard in nature; resolving to torment her no further, I stood up and went behind the turtle to move her, using the only safe handle nature had provided—her thick, scuted tail. The turtle shifted and turned her head slightly in an attempt to keep me in sight, but I knew that she could not possibly reach me with a strike from that angle or distance. This species must confront an enemy head-on, for it cannot shift its bulk around with anything resembling agility.

Bending down, I grasped the tail and gingerly hefted the monster aloft. I held the turtle at arm's length, facing away from me, since I knew she couldn't strike beneath herself, though she could have easily reached an unprotected knee or thigh if toted the other way around. Walking toward the road's edge and the rim of the marsh, I suddenly felt the snapper come to life. Finding herself, doubtless for the first time in her life, suspended head-down above dry land, the animal began to flail in heavy, slow-motion fury, the head lustily darting, the powerful jaws clapping repeatedly and futilely in thin air. She lunged and twisted, tossing herself about in frustrated, bewildered fury, completely unable to comprehend the nature of her predicament or to

A strictly manmade vista. *The flat, religiously manicured park lawn lies, ruglike and weed-free, behind the safety of a steel bulkhead that holds off the tides of the river beyond. The ornamental apple trees, contorted both by genetic design and by the prevailing winds of the nearby sea, offer blossom-fragrance and welcome shade to the picnickers who will appear later in the season. To the artist, however, the naked trees, branches just beginning to sprout tender leaflets, present an artistic challenge impossible to pass up.*

address it. The notion of an enemy that would assault her in such a manner was very far from her ancient, inherited menu of all possible threats and their appropriate responses.

In the midst of this huffing and puffing and snapping ordeal, as I was a mere foot or two from the roadside and the merciful end to this impromptu rescue obligation, I found myself pinned like a highway deer in the bright, unwelcome light of publicity.

A pickup pulled alongside; the youngish male driver leaned out the window. "Whaddya got there, a snapper?" I set the turtle down on the road, retaining a hold on her tail. "Yeah; big, isn't she?" The guy nodded slowly. 'Yeah—howddya know it's a she?" I lifted the turtle's tail a bit, indicated the location with a nod. "It's in the tail; the female's vent is closer to the end of the tail than the male's." The driver looked at me, still nodding slowly. "You mean you looked?" I suddenly felt very much like an idiot. "The females are the only ones you usually see wandering around on land—to lay their eggs," I said, vaguely irritated, and hoping fervently that this would do, and that I wouldn't have to stand here in the middle of a rain-swept road and explain turtle biology to a total stranger for very much longer. In silence, we both looked at the turtle; she was quiet, mouth still open, eyes glittering faintly in the streetlight's frosted glare. The rain whispered faintly along the road; the truck's wipers ka-wock-ka-wock-ka-wocked, filling the silence. "Whaddya goin' to do with 'her'?" he finally asked, shutting off the truck's engine (bad sign). "I was in the process of getting her off the road and back into the river," I said, hefting the turtle by her tail once more. "I'm getting soaked out here, so I'll seeya."

"Hey!" He stepped toward me, smiling with the sudden genesis of an idea. "I'll take her off your hands! Throw her in the back of the pickup here; I know a place, a restaurant, that'll buy her off me for soup, if you don't want her. That's a nice turtle."

I pondered the advisability of a roadside sermon on the place of snappers in the scheme of things. A snapping turtle has few friends in this world, and this young fellow didn't seem to be one of them. "I'll pass on the deal," I said, inspired in that direction by the feel of the suddenly very cold rain dripping off my nose and running down my neck. "I think she belongs back in the river; I wouldn't feel right just handing her over to be knocked off for soup. You know what I mean?" To my surprise, the kid did seem to know what I meant. He nodded, studying the giant creature intently; then he said something that surprised me. "You know, there don't seem to be many of them left, the big ones, and it's kinda good to know that they're still here, as ugly as they are. You know what I mean?"

It was my turn. I did know, only too well, that a crowded, thoroughly urbanized world empty of snappers would be seriously deficient, somehow, in just one of those numberless qualities that has always made it the special place it is and always has been to humans. There's something to be said for organization and regulation and perfect safety and sameness and efficiency in society, but not much, in my view, when you contemplate the

A thirty-foot white cedar, surrounded and almost enveloped by a mature poison ivy shrub. *This thicket, dense with foliage and quite secluded in the summertime, is situated right next to a popular fishing beach on the estuary, and eel and flounder anglers frequently avail themselves of its leafy privacy to "answer nature's call." None of the fishermen I've spoken to while angling there myself were aware of the shrub's notorious identity and properties, but from then on, they threaded their way into the tangle very gingerly indeed.*

A dirt road in New Jersey. *One of the few remaining dirt roads on the estuary gives an enigmatic, time-traveler's look at the Shark River that once was. This little "street," which descends to the bay shore from ever-busy West Sylvania Avenue in Neptune City is the frequent haunt of cottontail rabbits, which sun themselves undisturbed on the warm sandy soil of the roadbed. Shortly after I made this drawing, the town dumped a big load of fill dirt in the middle of the roadway, apparently an attempt to deny access to "midnight dumpers" who had been using the isolated spot as an illegal repository for rubble and refuse—a social problem certainly not restricted to the state of New Jersey.*

NIGHTFALL; THE UPPER RIVER; TURTLES ■ 155

loss. Nobody really "needs" a snapping turtle or would regret having never seen one, but just the knowledge that creatures like that are "still here" is oddly comforting.

We parted then, the driver and I, he with a wave of hand and a roar of engine and the wet spin of tires. His taillights vanished up the hill; the rain had passed on, and with the freshening breeze, ragged cloud cover raced to the northeast, the heavens appearing again in the dark sky. I turned to once again contemplate the turtle. She was moving across the remaining roadway, high on her legs in the manner of an alligator, toward the bank of the river. I followed, heard the faint, dragging whisk-whisk of the great, knobbed tail, watched the rocklike head bobbing with each slow, deliberate step. The turtle had forgotten me; her mind was already on other things, things that lay in the dark depths of the stream that moved flatly and inexorably toward the sea. She slid and scuffled down the muddy bank and plowed with a splash into the murky flow.

Part V

The Estuary; Drawing; Discoveries

Shark River snow scenes. *January 23, the first meaningful snowfall of the season blankets the estuary! But even with little more than an inch of accumulation, the snow-blow effects a transformation into one of stark beauty and uncommon contrasts. I decided to capture the essence of the riverine snowscapes in pen rather than pencil in order to better convey the subdued, duo-chromatic appearance of the frozen shoreline. For the purpose, I tried out a Faber-Castell "Uniball" pen with a 2mm tip and found that it gave me the fine detail I wanted in the drawings.*

*S*hark River is very close to being the consummate place of contrasts. In any given day more subtle changes and small happenings come to pass here, both within the natural sphere and among its human population, than in most other square miles of comparable territory on the North American continent. Much of this is integral with the presence and influence of the tidal cycle. The waters of the sea pour in through the channel, and the river is transformed into a placid bay; the ebb in turn arrives, and the place is exposed for what it really is: a broad parking and picnic ground for the gulls and countless other avian creatures of the littoral as the pungent mudflats are exposed to the sun.

People move over the estuary's surface in their watercraft and skirt its shoreline in their cars and on foot. The commuter trains of New Jersey Transit's North Shore Route rumble across the inlet's channel hourly. An aging bridge is buttressed and shored up, an old motel dismantled and razed, a new condo erected. A huge, nine-story high rise stands in imperious dominance on the Belmar skyline, while the sea labors patiently and endlessly to undermine many a lesser structure near the water's edge. The controversial issue of whether or not to dredge the harbor comes up, again, and is debated by the citizenry. Lobstermen set off into the predawn gloom, bound for the distant, offshore lumps; eelpotters chug about the little bay in their utilitarian, "seen better days" boats; the big, bright, air-conditioned party boat fleet sails daily from the Belmar Marina, loaded to the gunwales with angling hopefuls of nearly every race, religion, income bracket, and political persuasion. Great blue herons stalk the flats in sedate, if gawky majesty; herring, ring-billed, and laughing gulls patrol every inch of the shining plains and then some in airy, noisy freedom. Horseshoe crabs come ashore, out of the green depths, as they have for twenty times a millennium in maintaining their race in an increasingly treacherous world. In the dark waters below, a million times a million living things swarm, the marvelous minutiae of life.

The ocean, with its fragile, incredibly rich estuarine extension, is simply a part of the vast web of life that

Doves. *A foggy January day on the estuary's north arm offers a view best captured in soft pencil strokes. Mourning doves, a common coastal bird, seemed more abundant than usual in 1992, perhaps because of the steady and noticeable warming trend that allows them to find food in the generally inhospitable seaside environment.*

Osprey. *Leaving the beach at Memorial Park early one morning, I was taken by surprise by the sight of an osprey perched in the very top of one of the park's taller trees. The bird had a majestic look to it as it leaned into the brisk wind and gazed out over the wave-ridged estuary—its hunting ground and domain. This individual allowed a fairly close approach (close enough to work up a drawing without binoculars), leading me to think it was one of the year's young of the resident pair.*

oriented. Whatever else this thoroughly settled part of New Jersey may represent, its residents, as well as the seasonal tides of summer visitors, discover that their ultimate interest and orientation lies to the east: the ocean and its many nuances are at the heart of whatever allure and attraction the place has for people.

This multifaceted nature of the Shark River estuary, with all its many natural attributes and manmade warts,

embraces the planet as a whole, but in human terms, it is the reason that the convocations of people surrounding the estuary here at Shark River have taken on and to a considerable degree have retained the still unique character and flavor they have. In spite of the tide of development that has steadily overtaken the state as a whole and the Jersey shore area in particular, much of the essence of the coastal towns here is still very much summer-sea-sun

or gellow-rumped warblers.

A duo of myrtle, a.k.a. yellow-rumped warblers. *The birds were perched on a wind-tattered wax myrtle branch. Aside from the ever-abundant song sparrow, these sprightly little wood warblers are probably the commonest resident passerines of the seaside environment, often wintering in some numbers as far north as New York and Massachusetts. Their winter survival depends upon a plentitude of their favorite foods, the berries of their namesake plant, the wax myrtle, as well as those of the bayberry.*

A company of crows. *A small percentage of the army that patrols the estuary looks over the Memorial Park beach for edibles after a storm.*

has made it an endlessly fascinating object of interest for this particular artist and naturalist. I have traversed it both above and below the waterline, fished its beaches and bulkheads with eternal optimism, talked to many of its people, and just plain reveled in its many and varied moods, fair weather and foul. As with any natural habitat, in particular one in which the human presense plays so integral a part, the beginner with pad, pen, and pencil is well advised to be prepared for the unexpected, that small adventure that may appear right out of the blue and either enrich or complicate the experience. Surprises come in many guises; at Shark River they may appear thusly:

◀ **Wind and wave:** Both elementals are, of course, characteristic of the coastal environment and factors to be considered when wandering about with poised pad and pencil. The surf won't usually pose any real threat to a drawing rendered in nonwaterproof ink unless you have an exceptionally poor ability to gauge distance, but the waves can prove to be an enemy if they happen to be between you and dry land. Always familiarize yourself with the day's tide schedule when undertaking sketching forays out on slim sandspits or low jetties. More than once in my career I've had to swim for it when artistic or angling absorption allowed the sea to slip in behind me. Common sense would also dictate that when sketching anywhere near water or on a day with a questionable forecast, keep your pad snugly quartered in a large "Ziploc" pouch or in a waterproof totebag.

Conditions may be dead-calm a mile or two inland, but one can almost always count on a breeze at the shore—that's one of the hallmarks of the place. Wind is more of a nuisance than a real obstacle to drawing, but it can be downright uncomfortable when, for example, you're squatting down doggedly sketching the antics of a gang of ghost crabs on the beach and the persisent zephyrs are loaded with billions of tiny, airborne grains of sand! But for countering most wind conditions, the kinds that bring that unique, page-flapping irritation that every outdoor sketcher is familiar with, I find that a stout rubber band secures a rambunctious page with the least effort and hassle.

➤ Light: Sun glare and the resultant eyestrain can be a major problem in the littoral, what with all that nice flat, highly reflective sand, wet mud, and water. Sunglasses are the obvious solution to eye-tearing sunblindness, which can reach acute and painful proportions on a beach; the wonderfully reflective property of the paper itself doesn't help matters. I personally don't like to use shades for I find that they often obscure some

details in both the drawing and the subject. Instead, I'll often construct a makeshift sunshade out of my shirt or jacket and any long sticks or branches I can scour up in the vicinity. If that kind of disrobing and rummaging around isn't up your alley, lightweight, portable artist's "sunbrellas" are also available at most well-stocked art supplies stores. Keep in mind that in

Storm visitor. *As the second November oceanic storm in a week moved up the coast, bringing with it winds and rain and the threat of renewed flooding of coastal areas, all of the estuary's birds save the gulls seemed to vanish from sight. Cruising the shoreline just before the onslaught of the rain, I spotted this sparrow hawk, or kestrel, hunkered down on a leafless snag near the road, leaning into the rapidly freshening breeze and hoping for the best. I was able to use my van as a blind for the posing session, pulling the vehicle quite close to the little falcon, which swayed and blinked on its unsteady perch and absolutely refused to take wing into the gale.*

Beer can and shells; local beach. *The public-access beaches of the estuary are impacted to a considerable though varying degree by the litter eyesore. Perhaps understandably, the problem is more severe during the summer months, when trash is discarded by both beachgoers and boaters offshore.*

These natural and manmade artifacts were well up on the beach, at the highest spring tide line. The zone marks the edge of penetration by terrestrial plants; these tender shoots braving the wind and driven sand are young seaside goldenrod, a common and hardy seashore plant whose dense, tiny flowers lend a touch of yellow to the beach scene.

most field-sketching exercises you won't remain in one place long enough to warrant the building of an elaborate sunshade or shelter; the bugs, weather, or your subject's abrupt departure will ensure brevity in most instances!

✇ **Footgear:** Very unfortunately, adequate footgear is a must in most littoral situations today. With the exception of carefully maintained

bathing beaches and the wave-swept strands of oceanfront barrier islands, wandering about barefoot in coastal areas can be a risky pursuit. It is no shame at all for any state to admit that it has a "litter problem," for this nemesis has traveled everywhere that people have. The density of litter on the beaches of Shark River is no greater or less than on those that people frequent in Florida, Texas, or Alaska. Trash has found its way to the once pristine strands of tropical islets in the middle of the Pacific nowhere, refuse tossed from ships at sea.

For this reason, I always wear some sort of footgear, the nature of which is determined by the time of year. In summer, whether diving or simply wandering about on the beaches and flats, a worn pair of low-cut tennis shoes, sans socks, has served me well for the past five years. These afford good protection from most sharp, buried objects and can be rinsed of mud after each use and allowed to dry in the sun; even the blackest marsh mud generally flakes easily from fabric when it is bone-dry.

At other times of the year, stout work shoes are the best for travel in dry situations; noninsulated anglers' hip waders, worn over wool socks and folded down to the knee, will do the trick for sketching and exploring trips

Sleeping mallards. *This pair was spotted snoozing high on the beach, near a broad stand of brackish spartina grasses. One usually equates the mallard with freshwater habitats—park ponds in particular—but it is a very common duck up and down the New Jersey shore, where it competes with the coastal black duck for both nesting sites and mates. Although a true North American native, the mallard was originally confined to the central and prairie states. Those birds seen in the East are either the descendants of escaped domestic stock or true wild birds that have extended the natural range eastward.*

The female of this pair slept soundly through my entire drawing session, though her mate periodically raised his head to eye me suspiciously. The drawing was made with a Pilot razor-point pen.

involving any water entry. Waders should not be overly formfitting (read, "too tight"), for you never know when you may have to slip out of them in a hurry—for example, when you're caught in the vise-grip of a bottomless mudflat on an incoming tide.

➤ **Time and tide:** Time flies when you're having fun, and especially so by the beautiful sea. As noted earlier, the tide and its inexorable progress can make an impromptu swimmer out of the most nonathletic artist. Keep an eye on it, and, when field sketching from a

muscle-powered boat (a canoe, kayak, or rowboat), always anchor prior to becoming engrossed in working up a drawing. This cannot be stressed strongly enough, for a drifting boat may well be carried offshore or into heavily traveled boating lanes before the artist snaps back to the "real world' and grabs for the paddle or pull-cord. Exercise extreme care and prudence whenever operating a small boat anywhere near the sea—it is a friend to humans, but one with many and highly changeable moods and a misreading of tides and

Two studies of a few of the estuary's dedicated "watermen"—winter flounder anglers and sandworm diggers. *The artist should be prepared for mixed reactions when human subjects discover, as they usually do, that they are under artistic observation!*

sandworm diggers work the low tide mudflats.

weather can be fatal. The Coast Guard will be happy to regale you with some of their harrowing search-and-rescue stories if you offer to buy an off-duty round at a shoreside pub!

➤ **Bugs:** Coastal insects can, in a word, drive you buggy, especially in or near the salt and brackish marshes. When weather conditions are just right, they can be true man-eaters and are virtually unrivaled anywhere in the known universe for persistence and ferocity. The artist makes a delightfully unique victim: determined to finish that

2/18/92

A trio of horned grebes near a lobster dock investigating the bottom for edibles. *One bird is down, the other two on the surface, keeping an eye on me between dives. The sprightly little horned grebe is the commonest winter grebe on the estuary, outnumbering the pied-billed species ten to one; roughly forty to sixty appear to be resident on the estuary in an average winter.*

sketch before that coyly posed but jittery snowy egret flies away, he or she will effect some kind of weird, controlled, slow-motion swatting motions (to avoid spooking the subject), making agonized, jerky lines on the paper, and all the while emitting a string of low-decibel expletives and observations on the ultimate meaning of an artist's life.

Insect species, both biting and non, that frequent the littoral environment are far too numerous to list here, but some of the worst public enemies deserve at least passing mention:

Greenhead flies (Tabanus species): Devilishly determined and abundant little brutes in the salt-marsh habitat, greenheads can be a real problem on all but the windiest days. They do not readily respond to repellents and cannot be swatted with any degree of accuracy or success (they attack in legions), so the best defense is long sleeves and a wide-brimmed hat— mosquito netting in a real emergency. Greenheads seem oddly attracted to the still air inside parked automobiles, and a vehicle left parked with a window open will often be discovered to be filled

2/19/92
An un-natural shoreline: asphalt
and concrete rubble serve
buffer against bank erosion.
'ast these mallards find the
Atlantic!

Contrasts. *I'm not at all sure why I was prompted to record this piece of shoreline in pen; it was an especially dreary February day on the estuary. Fortunately, the pair of mallards were cooperative. This area was once, long ago, a small but productive swatch of salt marsh. In order to shore up the nearby road against storm tides, the shoreline was bermed-up and filled in with concrete rubble and asphalt, producing the lumpy, weed-spiked, unpromising-looking "beach" shown in the sketch. The mallard pair seemed quite unfazed by the grim surroundings and spent considerable time dabbling at the water line and "tipping up" in the shallows.*

2/26/92
coots and a single pied-billed
grebe paddle about a quiet
marina bay. one was walking
about on the floating boat.

Coots. Somehow, the combination of the jazzy name on the docked boat and the head-bobbing antics of the swimming coots seemed to make a visual statement about these entertaining birds. The coot is a member of the *Rallidae* and thus a close relative taxonomically of the slim, secretive rails and gallinules. But the relationship ends there, for the coot is a bold, inquisitive, almost clownish creature perfectly able to coexist among people at the shore. It is equally at home in the water or on land, where it struts about like a barnyard hen looking for food, even joining the jostling crowds of ducks and gulls being fed corn or bread by bird lovers.

with thousands of the little brutes—all furious and roaring about to find an escape route. Unless you're planning to move some distance from your car, leave all the windows wide open to allow them free ingress and egress. I can promise that you'll regret failing to follow this little piece of advice!

Deer flies: It is said that the best way to attract these flies is to run wildly about and wave one's arms energetically. This approach seems to work, but fortunately, deer flies are not nearly as plentiful as their green-eyed brethren. These flies usually attack singly or in pairs, so with practice it's possible to swat the intruders, thereby discouraging any comrades waiting in the wings.

Salt-marsh mosquitoes: These guys (or rather, girls, for only the females bite) are normally most active at dawn and dusk, so the best tactic is to do your salt-marsh sketching on bright windy

CROWS & STREET DRAIN

Crows and street drain. *There are a distressingly large number of both ancient and modern concrete street runoff drains—about 120 of them—scattered along the more developed beachfront of the estuary. These culverts, although not carrying sewage of any kind, do deliver road oils, litter, and other street contaminants to the bay.*

The drain outfalls seem to attract an abundance of both terrestrial and aquatic creatures in search of food items. Crows and gulls frequent the drain openings, and the low-tide sand is always intricately laced with raccoon, muskrat, and 'possum tracks. Killies and crabs are attracted to the freshwater flow, and plant growth in the brackish water is rather lush in the immediate vicinity.

It is something of an irony that in many East Coast estuaries, such human constructions as docks, bulkheads, and culverts are among the most productive "habitats" for the wildlife watcher and artist!

Kingfisher scanning for prey. *The belted kingfisher is never overly abundant on the estuary for it is an aggressive and territorial bird that does not tolerate the close proximity of others of its own kind. At Shark River, about four pairs share the roughly one-square-mile habitat of open water and shoreline, but even this area would not seem to provide enough elbow room, for there is always a lot of chasing and squabbling going on where the territories overlap.*

Kingfishers are chunky, bigheaded birds that spend a good deal of time perched on favored "lookouts," scanning the water for the smaller fish they eat.

This particular kingfisher favored the rugged wooden supports of a large culvert as its spotting perch, always returning to it after a "fishing trip" and fiercely driving off all interlopers that approached too closely. I drew it using a Bic razor-point pen.

days close to the noontime hour. Good, punky repellents work fairly well with these skeeters, though you may need a hat and netting on muggy, damp nights when they are especially aggressive.

Forget about organized swatting; there are always so many of them, and they're amazingly agile.

➤ **Drawing wildlife:** Sketching a stately maple is one thing; capturing a hyperactive wren scuttling through the branches of that maple is another matter altogether. The same can be said of a stand of seaside goldenrod and a scuttling of sanderlings on the ocean beach. One is a piece of cake, the other requires a fast eye and hand and considerable patience in securing that line impression.

Much of the natural scene at the estuary is stationary, that is, its broad natural features aren't going anywhere and can be sketched at relative leisure. But the creatures that live there are just as mobile, often erratically, unpredictably, and uncooperatively so, as are those in any other habitat. And often at the most inopportune times—such as at the precise moment you'd like them to "hold it!" One advantage of the "developed" nature of the Shark River ecosystem is that many, if not most, of the higher animals (the birds, in particular) that occur there are accustomed to the close proximity of people and have adjusted their behavior accordingly. It is thus possible to effect a quite close approach to many of the littoral birds, whether on foot or in a boat, with ample time to render a complete sketch. Often, simply

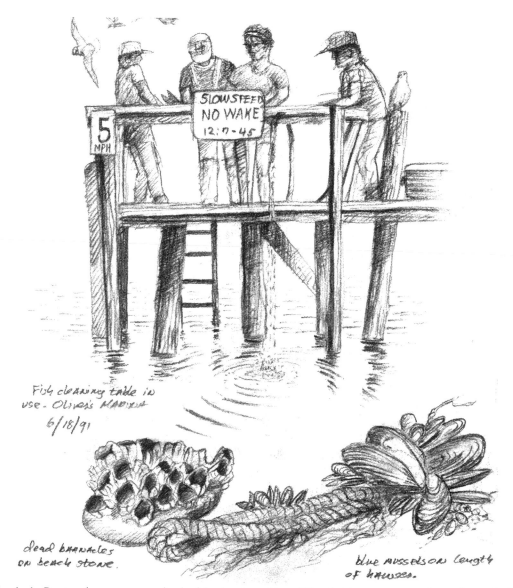

Fish cleaning table in
use - Oliver's Marina
6/18/91

dead barnacles
on beach stone.

blue mussels on length
of hawser.

At the dock. *During the summer months the fish-cleaning table at Oliver's Marina is a very busy place—both above and below the water's surface. Incoming, successful anglers dress the day's catch, attended by the usual collection of loafers and dockside superintendants, not to mention the ever-alert and hungry gulls. Below decks, the bottom beneath the dock is littered with "racks," the backbone and remains of cleaned fish, and these attract a multitude of scavengers. The majority of these are the blue, green, and hermit crabs, and the striped killifish and mummichog. Adding to the collection of debris are the usual human discards, such as cans and bottles plus sections of rope and metal, these usually festooned by mussels and barnacles. The barnacle-encrusted stone and overgrown hawser were found in shallow water at mean low tide. They amply illustrate that no solid object in the marine environment remains uncolonized by sea life for very long!*

Fish cleaning table at Oliver's marina
4/20/91

Fish-cleaning table at Oliver's Marina. *Oliver's, or the Shark River Hills Marina, is one of the busiest of the public anchorages during the summer months, and on weekends the filleting table is elbow-to-elbow with successful anglers from midafternoon on. During this period, the immediate surroundings are alive with gulls, crows, and other scavengers seeking cast-off fish offal. Needless to say, such a collection of avian panhandlers affords the bayside sketcher with limitless opportunities for securing excellent action drawings. The key here is to spend a good deal of time simply watching the birds in their milling flight and then attempt to very quickly rough in the general forms, to be finished later at leisure. Gulls waiting for scraps on the water or on the surrounding pilings allow for a much more methodical approach to sketching them.*

Semipalmated plovers; local beach. *These engaging little "beach birds" are closely related to the endangered piping plover, now under strict protection in New Jersey. The semipalmated is one of the first of the shorebird species to pass through the estuary on the way north in early spring; the birds form loosely organized flocks on the beaches and tidal flats where they energetically probe for all manner of invertebrate prey.*

These two individuals allowed a very close approach (to within about fifteen feet), and since they were concentrating on simply hunkering down in a very stiff west wind, they were loathe to fly and thus held their poses nicely. The sun was low in the west and behind the birds; thus they appear as silhouettes.

This drawing was executed with a Pilot Fineline pen; owing to the difficulties involved in controlling the pen— and the paper—in the strong wind, I roughed it in on the beach and finished it later. Steel clips or a stout rubber band to hold paper down are wise additions to your equipment package when going afield on windy days.

hunkering down on sand or tideflat and remaining as unthreateningly motionless as possible for a few minutes is all it takes to instill a sense of ease, as well as curiosity, among birds and encourage them to return to "business as usual."

Fishes and other aquatic creatures best sit for their portraits while temporarily confined in a portable, flat-sided container (curved glass distorts the image), such as a two- or five-gallon aquarium brought along for the purpose. They can be collected by any number of effective methods—from rod and reel through dip net, seine, or digging trowel—placed in the tank filled with bay water, and sketched at leisure. The same technique can be used for drawing marine algae and other delicate submarine plants; a plant that looks like a shapeless mass of greenish or reddish goo when held in the hand will unfold into a living object of lacy elegance when suspended in water, its natural medium.

The people factor: Here's where the fun begins, and often ends, on any field-sketching excursion. It's tempting for an artist to regard his or her fellow human beings as something of an annoyance and source of interruption, like benevolent mosquitoes, when encountered on a field-sketching foray; they're inhibiting of free expression (and conducive to mistake making); they ask too many questions; they usually offer a lot of unsolicited comments and suggestions about the work in progress—and all that sort of thing. But for better or worse, not only are people an integral part of the scene at Shark River, but they and their constructions and activities impart to the estuary the unique flavor it possesses.

Although I don't go out of my way to include people in my field sketches (I don't draw them particularly well), at a place like Shark River it's often

Neptune City's Memorial Park. *This is the archetypal town park, replete with marble veterans' monument and picnic area—except for one thing: it fronts on a tidal estuary and as the tide falls, its lovely white-sand beach slowly expands into acres and acres of mudflats. Memorial Park is actively utilized by the citizenry, though public swimming there is an on-again-off-again proposition, depending on the current fecal coliform count. The park's broad shorefront is a favorite resting spot for numerous shorebirds in spring and fall, and much of the estuary's sizable winter brant population often gathers on the low-tide flats for feeding and just plain loafing.*

A lush tangle of bittersweet, a common, weedy vine. *Bittersweet proliferates in a wide variety of habitats. Here it unfolds in the lee of a beach bulkhead in the May sunshine.*

detail of new leaves and flowers. MAY 20th

Long-rooted Shadbush

Shadbush. The "in's and out's" of coping with a chain link fence are addressed in an almost artistic way by this shadbush growing near the Memorial Park beach. This determined tree illustrates the slow-motion violence of nature in its forced rearrangement of the links in the fence. As a seedling and then young tree, it grew in and out through the links, spreading them and finally twisting them out of shape as the trunk put on girth. The arrangement doesn't seem to inconvenience the tree at all, though it doesn't do much for the fence. The likely end to this little scenario will be the eventual discovery of the fence damage by Parks Department crews and the eviction of the shadbush via chain saw. Unfortunate, perhaps, for there are few more unattractive and forbidding manmade constructions than an unadorned and sterile chain link fence.

Red cedar and bayberry thicket
The south arm of the estuary,
looking toward the town of Belmar
and the ocean. Male redwings are
on duty, setting up their territories.
April 9th, 92

Territorial boundaries. *A young red cedar and an ancient bayberry bush discuss botanical matters over a chain link fence on the south cove of the estuary, while a male red-wing blackbird exuberantly proclaims the boundaries of his spring territory to every other red-wing in the vicinity.*

"Twenty-knot, northwest wind." An eel fyke set marker stake and flag bows to the insistent force of a stiff offshore breeze, and a raft of herring gulls keep a low profile in between tides.

unavoidable and in fact desirable, since so much of the "doings" there involve human as well as animal activity. The question of how to handle the people-sketching issue is an interesting one, involving not a small amount of diplomacy. Unlike nature, human subjects notice that they are the object of an artist's attention and react in various ways. The great majority are flattered when informed of their status as "models"; others are not. I once sat on

the beach at what I thought was a respectable distance from a group of worm diggers on the mudflat, recording their activity in pen (see sketch). For most of the production of the sketch, they were unaware of my presence, but at one point, one of them saw me and informed the others. They kept digging but were clearly unnerved by the sight of a man looking intently in their direction and then jotting things down in a notebook. I didn't have the good

7:30 AM Aug. 19
HURRICANE Bob APPROACHES.

A Rising wind - but no Rain as yet -
keeps some of the Resident gulls on the
water, while some stay Awing.

Hurricane Bob arrives, August nineteenth, 7:30 A.M. *The first major tropical storm to strike the estuary this year, Bob began to make its presence felt just before dawn. High winds swept out of the northeast, driving low, ragged clouds before them; surprisingly, a good number of gulls and terns were nonchalantly airborne as the hurricane approached the New Jersey coast. They fought against the wind's power with deep, rowing strokes of the wings, seeming to savor the exhilaration of breasting the natural forces and the capability of their own wings.*

This was before the rain arrived. When the storm descended upon the estuary in full force, the sixty-mile-an-hour winds and driving rain quickly emptied the sky of birds. Within minutes, the gulls in the hundreds were seen hunkered down on protected beaches and flats in the lee of the northern shorelines. Even there, they were fully exposed to much of the hurricane's force, though given their marvelous covering of watertight feathers and ability to "read" the nature of the elements, they were able to lean into the wind and weather the storm.

sense to wander over and introduce myself, and finally one of them irritably jammed his fork into the mud and approached me with obvious hostile intent. His two companions stood and watched. I rose as he came right up to me and indicated my pad with a curt nod. "Whaddya writin'?" I replied with what I hoped was a disarming smile, "I'm an artist, and I'm just sketching scenes on the river—for a book." He wasn't completely mollified by the response. "What kinda book—you're not a game warden?" "Not at all," I assured him. "You guys just looked, well, picturesque digging out there. Here, take a look."

The man softened, waved the others over; leaving their gear out on the flats, they all studied my assemblage of sketches with mild, cautious interest. I never did ask them why they were concerned that I was a game warden; in view of the high degree of Fish and Game surveillance of the area and what I knew went on out on the flats, I just didn't think it was a good idea.

In the long run, I've related to the people of Shark River, whether they be weather-beaten local anglers and bait diggers, tender-palmed summer sailors, or the clerks at the nearby Wawa or Cracker Barrel, simply as fellow visitors to this little part of the coast and thus as much a part of it as I. Many of the local folk know me by sight and have at least a general idea of what I'm up to when they see me prowling about the mudflats and beaches with a net or sketch pad at the ready. All seaside passersby, whether aquaintance or total stranger, have expressed interest in the proceedings at hand.

Why field sketch? What's the rationale behind going afield, braving wind, rain, and blazing sun, hunched over a little loose-leaf pad, its pages furiously aflap in the gale, to produce a series of rough little studies of generally uncooperative wildlife subjects?

In short, just what constitutes a field sketch, and why do artists, of just about any artistic persuasion, find so much pleasure in producing it?

In theory, the field sketch, otherwise and sometimes known as a "working drawing," is usually executed as part of the production of a finished painting or illustration. At least, that's generally been the case with this particular artist. Many artists, nature artists in particular, produce field sketches for the sheer joy of it and over the years assemble vast, loose-leaf tomes of them that may outweigh a century's worth of *National Geographics.* Often such "impressions" created in the field are to be combined or refined and rendered into something worth gracing a book page or a gallery wall. This is especially true for artists who either make a living at their art or at least try to.

Sun and shadow. *A sturdy sapling hangs on at the edge of a sand bank at the Memorial Park beach. The bright midafternoon sun, white sand, and the intricate, spidery shadows of the plants appealed to me, and I was in the process of wrapping up the sketch when this fish crow alighted on the piling stub, leaned into the west wind, and began calling lustily out over the bay. The perfect accent to the drawing!*

This sketch is a prime example of the technique of deliberately omitting details in the interest of simplicity and clarity in a drawing; a dense, tangled stand of trees was directly behind the sand bank, but its inclusion in the rendering would have made the piece too dark and confusing so I left it out—not even a suggestion of tree line.

A first-year black-backed gull. *Though secure in its size and ability to fly, this bird keeps a cautious eye on a nearby artist.*

okeweed against
10/3/91 old bulkhead

An assembly of "weeds" gracing a piling bulkhead on the upper beach. *Shown here are two of the hardiest plant invaders of the disturbed environment: pokeweed (Phytolacca americana) thickets nestle against the base of the stout wood, while in the foreground, the ever-cosmopolitan crabgrass (Digitaria sanguinalis) ekes out a living in the sandy environment of the beach itself.*

By its very definition, a field sketch is just that—a simple rendering made "on site" without pretensions or the prospect of pleasing anyone but oneself. It can be little more than a few lines that merely suggest the gross form of the subject being viewed, or, depending on the degree of finishing involved, take on the appearance of a detailed lithograph.

The dictionary defines the word "sketch" as "a hasty or undetailed drawing or painting made as a preliminary study." The first object of the field sketch is to capture the basic essence of the animal subject and its surroundings. This almost always involves a "hasty and undetailed" rendering indicating basic form and the suggestion of the immediate environment. This first stage is, in fact, the "preliminary study" and can be touched up and refined later; as noted earlier, no one knows for sure when a field sketch metamorphoses into a finished drawing, but in general, when the degree of detail and overall "tightness" of the piece becomes obvious, giving the work the look and feel of studio art, it is no longer a field sketch.

Although one usually thinks "hand-held sketch pad and carbon pencils" in any discussion of the art of field sketching, in fact, a wide variety of media may be used. Newsprint, vellum paper, parchment, and even stiff bristol board have all been pressed into service by artists, and while all will essentially produce the desired effect, the conventional sketch pad is normally a medium-toothed rag paper of off-white color. Standard, No. 2 bonded lead pencils may be used, though these may produce a rather pale effect lacking in the texture that lends visual appeal to a field sketch. Though I certainly use ordinary pencils with good results, I generally prefer Wolf carbon pencils of English manufacture; these are available in varying degrees of hardness, with the H 838 grade being my own particular favorite. This grade permits a considerable degree of soft shading yet is hard enough to retain a good point for detail work without endless sharpening. I effect and maintain the desired point using a utility knife and sandpaper pad; in emergencies, the point can simply be rolled on a handy hard surface—such as the boulder serving as your perch in the field.

In the matter of the ink field sketch, an approach I've increasingly come to favor over pencil, my three favorite weapons are the Faber-Castell 2mm Uniball pen, the Pilot razor-point pen, and the Pentel Micro Permaroller, of Japanese maunfacture. These pens, readily available in any well-stocked stationery store or pharmacy, offer a superfine line, and after having done some time on the field-sketch circuit, they begin to run a bit "sketchy" and produce an intriguing and attractive "dry brush" feel to drawings.

Beyond the essential materials, a few other items may serve to make the field sketching trip a more pleasant and productive one. A beach umbrella or, at the least, a pair of sunglasses will serve to deflect the eyestraining brilliance of the white page on a sunlit summer beach; flat metal clips or at best a stout rubber band are an indispensable aid in thwarting the evil intentions of the sea wind; and a suitably sized canvas tote bag serves admirably as an equipment depository in the event of a rain squall's sudden appearance out of the blue.

As noted earlier, I generally select material for field sketching on the

The ketch. *Sometimes the key to the successful drawing is knowing when to quit. A drawing may be as intricate and involved as the scene demands, or it may be quite simple. I had stopped by Memorial Park early one foggy morning and was taken by the sight of a small ketch anchored on the "flat-calm" waters of the bay. The boat appeared to simply hang in space, anchored to the planet solely through its reflection in the water. The combination of pale early-morning sun and sea-fog diffused the quiet little scene into a most beautiful, misty, pastel effect.*

basis of whether it is suitable to the production of finished art of one kind or another. However, on many occasions over the years I have been in a position to capture "once in a lifetime" wildlife experiences on paper simply because I make it a point to carry my pad and pencils with me in my vehicle wherever I go.

Drawing in the field, outdoors in your square mile, should be as free of encumbrances and disciplines as possible. It should not be labored in any shape, manner, or form, but, rather, reflect the same wisdoms and passions of such outdoor pursuits as birding, hiking, and general nature study. Beyond the really minimal (and inexpensive) roster of equipment, the only other requirements of this fascinating and thoroughly enjoyable artistic persuasion are a love of the outdoors and its inhabitants and a desire to know and record them. The rest—the ability to render in two dimensions a faithful impression of what you see and enjoy—will become as natural as breathing!

Appendix

FLORA AND FAUNA OF THE SHARK RIVER ESTUARY

Habitats: Coastal marine; shallow-water estuarine; brackish marsh; riverine forest; suburban.

THE MAMMALS

MARINE
Humpback whale (occ., visible from shore)
Finback whale (occ., visible from shore)
Bottlenose dolphin (occ. in summer)
Harbor seal (occ. in winter)
Hooded seal (rare in winter; two records)

TERRESTRIAL
Raccoon
Striped skunk
Virginia opossum
Red fox (uncommon)
Gray fox (uncommon)
White-tail deer (resident in Shark River Park)
Gray squirrel
Woodchuck (fields and highway verges)
Norway rat (common around docks and jetties)
Muskrat
House mouse
White-footed mouse
Meadow vole

Eastern cottontail
Big brown bat
Little brown myotis
Red bat

THE BIRDS
Note: One asterisk (*) means that the bird was observed in fall and winter; two asterisks (**) denote a shorebird observed in fall and spring.

LITTORAL/ESTUARINE
Common loon *
Red-throated loon *
Horned grebe *
Pied-billed grebe *
Brown pelican (occ.)
Northern gannet *
Great cormorant (occ.)
Double-crested cormorant
Great blue heron
Green-backed heron
Cattle egret (occ.)
American (great) egret
Snowy egret
Black-crowned night heron
Yellow-crowned night heron (rare)
Least bittern (rare)
American bittern (uncommon)

Glossy ibis (occ.)
Mute swan (occ.)
Canada goose
Brant *
Snow goose (occ.) *
Mallard
Black duck
Gadwall *
Northern pintail *
Blue-wing teal (uncommon)
American wigeon (baldpate) *
Eurasian wigeon (rare) *
Canvasback *
Redhead (occ.) *
Ring-necked duck *
Greater scaup *
Lesser scaup (occ.) *
Common goldeneye *
Bufflehead *
Oldsquaw *
Harlequin duck (rare.) *
Common eider (occ.) *
White-winged scoter (uncommon) *
Surf scoter *
Black scoter (uncommon) *
Ruddy duck *
Hooded merganser (upper river) *
Red-breasted merganser *
Semipalmated plover **
Killdeer
Piping plover (rare; endangered)
Lesser golden plover (rare) **
Black-bellied plover **
Whimbrel (occ.) **
Greater yellowlegs **
Lesser yellowlegs **
Solitary sandpiper **
Spotted sandpiper
Ruddy turnstone **
Common snipe (occ.) **
Short-billed dowitcher **

Red knot **
Sanderling **
Semipalmated sandpiper *
Least sandpiper **
White-rumped sandpiper *
Western sandpiper *
Baird's sandpiper (rare) *
Purple sandpiper *
Dunlin *
Glaucous gull *
Great black-backed gull
Herring gull
Ring-billed gull
Laughing gull
Bonaparte's gull *
Black-legged kittiwake (occ. pelagic) *
Forster's tern
Common tern
Arctic tern (occ. pelagic)
Roseate tern (rare)
Least (little) tern (occ.)
Royal tern (occ.)
Caspian tern (occ.)
Black skimmer (occ.)
Thick-billed murre (occ.) *

LITTORAL AND UPLAND
Turkey vulture
Sharp-shinned hawk *
Red-tailed hawk
Broad-winged hawk *
Bald eagle (rare)
Northern harrier (occ.)
Osprey (about four in residence)
Peregrine falcon (occ.)
Merlin (occ.)
Kestrel (sparrow hawk)
Ring-necked pheasant
Bobwhite (uncommon)
Clapper rail
Virginia rail (occ.)

American coot *
Common gallinule (moorhen)
Rock dove
Mourning dove
Yellow-billed cuckoo (occ.)
Black-billed cuckoo (rare)
Barn owl
Great horned owl (rare)
Snowy owl (rare) *
Long-eared owl (rare) *
Short-eared owl (rare) *
Common screech owl (uncommon)
Whip-poor-will (occ.)
Chimney swift
Ruby-throated hummingbird (occ.)
Belted kingfisher
Northern flicker
Hairy woodpecker
Downy woodpecker
Eastern kingbird
Horned lark
Tree swallow
Barn swallow
Purple martin (uncommon)
Blue jay
American crow
Fish crow
Carolina chickadee
Tufted titmouse
White-breasted nuthatch
Red-breasted nuthatch
House wren
Winter wren (rare)
Carolina wren
Marsh wren (uncommon)
Cedar waxwing
Northern mockingbird
Gray catbird
Brown thrasher
American robin
Wood thrush (occ.)

Hermit thrush
Ruby-crowned kinglet
Golden-crowned kinglet
Northern shrike (rare)
Starling
Red-eyed vireo
Yellow-rumped (myrtle) warbler
Yellow warbler
Common yellowthroat
Black-and-white warbler
Ovenbird (occ.)
House sparrow
Red-wing blackbird
Northern (Baltimore) oriole
Common grackle
Boat-tailed grackle
Brown-headed cowbird
Scarlet tanager
Northern cardinal
Purple finch
House finch
American goldfinch
Seaside sparrow
Dark-eyed (slate-colored) junco
Chipping sparrow
White-throated sparrow
Fox sparrow (uncommon) *
Savannah sparrow **
Swamp sparrow
Song sparrow
Lapland longspur (rare)
Snow bunting

REPTILES AND AMPHIBIANS

Note: Virtually no reptiles or amphibians are to be found within my square mile of the estuary because it is a saline environment inhospitable to this group of animals; the endemic, salt-tolerant diamondback terrapin is very rarely seen and has likely been extirpated. The degree of development in the Shark River area as a whole has greatly reduced the diversity of the herptofauna, but the following animals may still be found here in varying degrees of abundance, even within suburbanized areas.

Snapping turtle (common in the upper river)

Eastern painted turtle (common in the park lake)

Diamondback terrapin (rare, probably extirpated)

Eastern box turtle (fairly common but declining)

Smooth green snake (occ. in wooded areas)

Brown (Dekay's) snake (common)

Eastern garter snake (common)

Northern water snake

Bullfrog

Green frog (common in Shark River Park)

Northern Leopard frog

Fowler's toad

Spring peeper (surprisingly common)

Northern cricket frog (rare, declining)

Gray treefrog

Red-backed salamander

FISHES

Note: The inventory does not include pelagic fishes, such as the tunas, or sharks occurring off the coast of New Jersey. Although no freshwater forms occur within the square mile of the estuary itself, the common eel, the hogchoker, and the mummichog may occupy both habitats. The common sunfish (pumpkinseed), golden shiner, banded killifish, tessalated darter, and other fishes occurring in the upper river may venture into brackish waters with salinities up to at least ten parts per thousand.

An asterisk (*) denotes a summer transient.

Spiny dogfish (common inshore)

Little skate

Clearnose skate

Bluntnose stingray (occ. in summer)

Shortnosed sturgeon (rare, endangered)

Cownose ray

American eel

Conger eel

Blueback herring

Atlantic herring

Alewife

Atlantic menhaden (bunker)

Bay anchovy

Inshore lizardfish

Gafftopsail catfish (uncommon)

Oyster toadfish

Atlantic tomcod

Red hake (ling)

Atlantic needlefish

Atlantic saury (uncommon inshore)

Sheepshead minnow

Rainwaterfish (rainwater killy)

Mummichog

Spotfin killifish (occ. in salt marshes)

Striped killifish

Banded killifish (in upper river)

Eastern mosquitofish (occ. in upper river)

Rough silverside

Atlantic silverside

Deepwater squirrelfish *

Bluespotted cornetfish *

Fourspine stickleback

Three-spine stickleback (uncommon)

Northern pipefish

Lined sea horse (cyclic in abundance)

White perch

Striped bass

Black sea bass

Bigeye *

Short bigeye *

Bluefish (snapper, chopper)

Bar jack *
Crevalle jack *
Mackerel scad *
Bigeye scad *
Rough scad *
Lookdown *
Banded rudderfish *
Florida pompano *
Permit *
Gray snapper *
Sheepshead (porgy)
Pinfish *
Jolthead porgy
Scup
Northern kingfish
Spot (sea bream, lafayette)
Weakfish
Red goatfish *
Spadefish
Foureye butterflyfish *
Spotfin (common) butterflyfish *
Banded butterflyfish *
Reef butterflyfish (rare) *
Queen angelfish *
Blue angelfish *
Gray angelfish (infrequent) *
Sergeant major *
Beaugregory *
Bicolor damselfish (rare, one state record) *
Tautog (blackfish)
Cunner (bergall)
Striped mullet *
White mullet *
Northern sennet *
Northern stargazer
Striped blenny
Ocean pout
American sand lance (sand eel)
Naked goby
Tidewater goby (occ.)
Northern searobin

Atlantic mackerel (small spikes, tinkers, inshore)
Little sculpin (grubby)
Summer flounder (fluke)
Sundial (windowpane, sand dab)
Winter flounder (blackback)
Hogchoker (sole)
Unicorn filefish (uncommon)
Orange filefish (foolfish) *
Scrawled filefish *
Planehead (gray) filefish
Queen triggerfish *
Scrawled cowfish (rare) *
Northern puffer (blowfish)
Striped burrfish *
Ocean sunfish (stranded specimen in harbor)

INVERTEBRATES

Note: The invertebrates are by far the most numerous, both in families and genera (many hundreds) as well as in sheer numbers, and a complete listing would tax the patience of all but the most determined reader. This listing is thus a condensed roster of the various organisms found here; many are those I've personally observed or studied, while the remainder are known to occur in the estuary.

Organpipe sponge
Finger sponge
Crumb-of-bread sponge
Red beard sponge (Microciom)
Lion's mane (red jellyfish)
Sea nettle
Moon jellyfish
Leidy's jellyfish
Dead man's fingers
Star coral (stony coral)
Frilled anemone (Metridium)

Striped anemone
Ghost anemone
Sea gooseberry (sea walnut)
Parchment worm (*Chaetopterus*)
Creeping bryozoan species
Red crusts (red bryozoans)
Lacy crust bryozoan (*Conopeum*)
Common periwinkle
Smooth periwinkle
Lobed moon shell
Northern moon shell
Oyster drill
Mud dog whelk (nassa snail)
Channeled whelk (*Busycon*)
Solitary glassy bubble (bubble shell)
Salt-marsh snail
Seaweed snails (*Hydrobia*)
Sea slug (emerald sea slug)
Striped nudibranch
Eastern chiton (*Chaetopleura*)
Veiled clam
Ponderous ark
Blue mussel
Ribbed mussel
Bay scallop (rare)
Common oyster (nearly extirpated)
Jingle shell
Chestnut astarte
Quahog (hard clam, littleneck)
Surf clam (*Spisula*)
Macoma clam
Stout tagulus (short razor clam)
Common razor clam
Soft-shell clam (gaper, piss clam)
Angelwing
Shipworm (*Teredo*)
Long-finned squid (larvae in estuary)
Bloodworms (*Glycera*)
Clam worms (*Nereis*)
Atlantic horseshoe crab
Booted fish lice (*Caligus*)

Northern rock barnacle
Ivory barnacle
Bay barnacle
Greedy isopod
Gribble (*Limnoria*)
Big-eyed amphipod
Beach fleas (*Talorchestia*)
Scuds (*Gammarus*)
Skeleton shrimp (*Caprella*)
Mysid shrimp
Shore (grass) shrimp (*Palemonetes*)
Sand shrimp
Grass shrimps (*Hippolyte*)
Long-clawed hermit crab
Flat-clawed hermit crab
Mole crab
Common (nine-spined) spider crab
Six-spined spider crab (uncommon)
Rock crab
Green crab
Blue crab
Lady (calico) crab
Black-fingered mud crab
White-fingered mud crab
Marsh crab (*Sesarma*)
Ghost crab (occ. on oceanfront beaches)
Fiddler crab (*Uca*)
Hairy sea cucumber
Purple sea urchin
Green sea urchin (occ.)
Sand dollar (occ.)
Forbes' Asterias (common sea star, starfish)
Short-spined brittlestar
Golden star tunicate
Sea grapes (tunicates, sea squirts)
Salps

Plants

Marine Plants; Inshore and Estuarine Algae

Green fleece (*Codium*)
Sea lettuce (*Ulva*)
Green sea fern (*Bryopsis*)
Sausage weed (*Scytosiphon*)
Knotted wrack (uncommon)
Rockweeds (*Fucus*)
Sea oak (*Phycodrys*)
Lacy red weed (*Gracilaria*)
Brushy red weed
Crustose algae
   Calothrix (red-brown)
   Vaucheria (green)
   Lithophyllum (white-red)
   Petroclis (bright red)
Filamentous algae
   Ulothrix (green)
Seed plants
   Eelgrass (tapegrass) (*Zostera*)
   Wigeon (ditch) grass (*Ruppia*)

Terrestrial Plants

Note: These are the representative plants of the rather limited beachfront/dunes complex, the brackish marsh, the remnant riverine hardwood forest, and the disturbed, "suburban" environment that surrounds the estuary.

Beaches/dunes

American beach grass (often replanted by
   humans)
Sea oats
Seaside goldenrod
Dusty miller
Short dune grass
Sea rocket
Seaside spurge
Russian thistle (common on bay beaches)
Cocklebur (*Xanthium*)
Sand bur
Switchgrass (*Panicum*)
Beach bean
Pin weed
Seabeach sandwort
Beach heather
Poverty grass
Beachpea (*Lathyrus* species)
Winged pigweed
Jointweed (*Polgonella*)

Brackish marsh

Salt grass (spike grass)
Black needle rush
Seabeach orach
Black grass
Saltwort (*Salicornia*, glasswort)
Sea lavender
Sea blite
Salt-marsh aster
Marsh pink
American threesquare rush
Salt-marsh bulrush
Marsh mallow
Big cordgrass (*Spartina alterniflora*)
Salt meadow hay (*Spartina patens*)
Water hemp
Germander
Phragmites (reed, plume grass, foxtail)
Wild morning glory

Trees and shrubs

Red maple
Sugar maple
Pitch pine
Willow
American holly
Bay berry

Wax myrtle
Sassafras
Wild black cherry
Osage orange
Black locust
Red cedar
Black alder
Scrub oak
Northern red oak
White oak
Staghorn sumac
Winged sumac
Smooth sumac

Vines and herbs

Note: Most of these species are plants typical of the disturbed habitat, in this case, the area's suburban character and the spoil and fill behind bulkheads and seawalls.

Virginia creeper
Poison ivy
Bullbriar
Summer grape
Ragweed
Butterfly weed
Common thistle
Sedge (*Cyperus*)
Queen Anne's lace
Jimson weed
Crabgrass
Buttonweed
Horseweed
Everlasting
Pokeweed
Slender-leaved goldenrod
Rabbitfoot clover
Wooley mullein

Bibliography

Berry, Thomas. *The Dream of the Earth.* San Francisco: Sierra Club Books, 1988.

Breder, C. M., Jr. *Fieldbook of Marine Fishes of the Atlantic Coast.* New York: Putnam's, 1929.

Carson, Rachel. *The Edge of the Sea.* Boston: Houghton Mifflin, 1955.

Cottrell, Richard F. *The Borough of Neptune City, N.J.: A Centennial History.* Neptune City: TFH Publications, 1981.

Coulombe, Deborah A. *The Seaside Naturalist.* Englewood Cliffs, N.J.: Prentice-Hall, 1984.

Cunningham, John T. *This Is New Jersey.* New Brunswick: Rutgers University Press, 1953.

Fox, William T. *At the Sea's Edge.* Englewood Cliffs, N.J.: Prentice-Hall, 1984.

Gillespie, Angus Kress, and Michael Aaron Rockland. *Looking for America on the New Jersey Turnpike.* New Brunswick: Rutgers University Press, 1989.

Gosner, Kenneth L. *A Field Guide to the Atlantic Seashore.* Boston: Houghton Mifflin, 1979.

Lippson, Alice J., and Robert L. Lippson. *Life in the Chesapeake Bay.* Baltimore: Johns Hopkins University Press, 1984.

Lyons, Janet, and Sandra Jordan. *Walking the Wetlands* New York: Wiley, 1989.

Manley, Robert, and Seon Monley. *Beaches.* Philadelphia: Chilton, 1982.

Miers, Earl Schenck. *Down in Jersey.* New Brunswick: Rutgers University Press, 1973.

Neptune City Historical Commission. *Four Score and Five: The History of Neptune City and Environs.*

Quinn, John R. *Our Native Fishes.* Woodstock, Vt.: Countryman Press, 1990.

Ricciuti, Edward R. *The Beachwalker's Guide.* Garden City, N.Y.: Doubleday, 1982.

Roberts, Mervin F. *The Tidemarsh Guide.* New York: Dutton, 1979.

———. *The Tidemarsh Guide to Fishes.* Old Saybrook, Conn.: Saybrook Press, 1985.

Rusher, Matthew J. "Shark River." Journalism paper, Temple University, Philadelphia, 1991.

Silberhorn, Gene M. *Common Plants of the Middle Atlantic Coast.* Baltimore: Johns Hopkins University Press, 1982.

Stalter, Richard. *Barrier Island Botany.* Sandy Hook, N.J.: Eastern National Park and Monument Association, n.d.

van Deventer, Fred. *Cruising New Jersey Tidewater.* New Brunswick: Rutgers University Press, 1964.

Index